SCANDALOUS NEW ORLEANS

SCANDALOUS NEW ORLEANS

An Encyclopedia of Crime, Prostitution, Corruption, Loose
Ladies, Gamblers, and Crooked Politicians

By

Fred deClouet

2878 Forest Street, Denver, CO 80207
Printed in U.S.A.

About the Book

While the book's main focus is on crime, gambling, prostitution and crooked politicians it also goes to great length in detailing the economic and social aspects of a complex society.

Most visitors to the old city are confused by the many gradations of skin colors and how race - identification is determined. The Negro's status grew in direct proportion to the whiteness of his skin color. The book includes a table listing the various mixtures of skin colors and defining them e.g Mullato, Quadroon Octooon.

Vooddooism and Mardi Gras is dealt with extensively, two of the many reasons why New Orleans is Known as "America's most interesting city," and at the same time the "wickedest city on earth"

Table of Contents

Foreword

To anyone who has never been to new Orleans during Mardi Gras time, here, through the eyes of a young boy, is a knot hole peek.

It's shortly after sunrise in New Orleans. Tall old houses are yet not awake on their narrow streets. A middle-aged man and a small boy are going together to the French Market for coffee. They have come from the Southern Pacific Railroad train station having just arrived from Albania Plantation some one-hundred and twenty miles south west of New Orleans. Already the boy is intoxicated with the strange new scent of the city, different from the sweet familiar smell of the country. The uneven cobblestone makes it difficult for the boy to walk. As they approach the market, he looks curiously at the slate-covered roof supported by brick pillars. Under the arcade masses of people moving about and the building buzzes like a hive of bees.

Wagons pass by loaded with cabbages, carrots, lettuce and tomatoes. Drivers, with their whips cracking, beat their horses. Both men and women pushing and shoving for positions to bargain with the vegetable sellers. Old Negro women with bright-stripped tignons on their heads and with baskets on their arms wander through the crowd buying a little of this and a little of that. Fruit is piled high. Two nuns wearing blue robes and stiff white headpieces are buying a bunch of bananas.

A Negro man passes with a flat basket filled with pink roses upon his head, whistling as he goes by. An old Indian woman, wrapped in a blanket, is selling red and green striped baskets. Near her, two Italian children crouched beside a crumbling brick pillar warming their hands over a charcoal furnace, a skinny black dog runs by with a piece of raw meat in his mouth. A cat with a little bell around its neck arches its back and hisses like a snake.

This is nothing like the plantation, thought the boy. And there in the midst of all this confusion is the coffee house, between the stalls of fruit and vegetables. The man and the boy sit upon stools drinking hot black coffee together and soon there are little honey flavored cakes still warm from the oven. The man, who is the boy's mother's uncle, smiles and nods contentedly at peace with the world. But the boys eyes were busy watching and listening. Around the market men are talking and drinking coffee. The boy hears the different languages being spoken. It is all new, strange and exciting.

Finishing their coffee and cakes, the man and boy continue on their way. They go past butchers' stalls with their slabs of beef, and rabbits hanging upside down. They next enter the fish market where thousands of fish are hanging on hooks and piled in baskets quivering. Great baskets are filled with blue and green crabs, their claws continuously wavering. Other baskets are filled with green shrimp. Some of the crabs have managed to escape and are moving about the floor. A boy in a dirty white apron catches them with tongs and throws them back in the basket. A man comes by with about twenty red fish, each one strung through its mouth with palmetto leaf. As he enters the fish stalls, he throws his shuddering burden on a table with their tails flopping at irregular intervals. Outside on the sidewalk is a flower market with many plants; roses, ferns, little trees filled with blood-red round peppers. Many of the Negroes and white men have flowers stuck behind their ears or in their caps.

An old beggar woman with wild white hair reclines upon the stone floor leaning back against a brick pillar, her crutch beside her. She is eating a bunch of grapes and spitting out the seeds at a white rooster which lies there, its feet tied together with a red rag. The old woman looks so witch-like. The boy comes closer with eyes wide open, half hoping, half fearing she will suddenly ride away on a broomstick.

He is quite close before the old woman looks up and sees him; she gives him a big smile and says, "Well, young man, where did you come from all of a sudden?". The boy answers politely, "I came from Albania Plantation, that's close to Jeanerette, on the Bayou Tech. I just got here." "Well, you don't happen to have a nickel for me, do you?" The boy's great-uncle drops a coin into her hand. She looks at it, smiles, and says,

"May all the Saints bless you for it," and then in a friendly whisper to the boy, "I hope you enjoy yourself." "Thank you," says the boy, "I will."

And this was my first impression of the city, I learned to love when I went there with my great-uncle Gaston (Sam) Richards more than sixty years ago. The trip had very special significance for both of us. For Uncle Sam it meant fulfilling a promise he made to his niece (my mother) two years after I was born - that he would take me to New Orleans one day when I was older for a very special occasion. For me it was the celebration of a special occasion, my birthday! For you see, I was born on a Mardi Gras Day and my middle name is Rex, which I refuse to use. Leaving the French Market area, we went down a narrow street leading away from the river toward the center of the city.

As we passed through the street, women were washing the banquettes (sidewalks) by pouring pails of water in swishes and sweeping it off. Other women were scrubbing wooden steps with pounded red brick dust. They called it reddenin. An old Negro woman passed by dressed in blue and wearing a stiff white apron. She carried a covered basket crying out monotonously, "Callas? Callas?"

Somewhere on Orleans Street, just off Royal Street, my uncle stopped before a heavy door and raised the iron knocker and let it fall. As we were waiting, two nuns passed by walking slowly with heads bowed down. I could see one was black with the whitest teeth I had ever seen.

Presently, the door opened and a large Negro woman stood aside that we might enter, and we went in. The passage into which we had come was about fifty feet long and about fifteen feet wide. At the end of the passage, seen through an arch of masonry, was a large court yard in which bamboo and tall palm trees grew. There was a fountain in the center.

The whole courtyard was full of color and near the fountain sat an old man in black near a small table laid in the open air. The old man was clearly surprised and overjoyed upon seeing my uncle. He embraced him, which I thought extremely odd. Men shook hands in those days. They did not embrace. They then began to converse in French, which I am sure was more comfortable for them than English.

The old woman who had let us in was now mopping the long passageway.

Coming back to the conversation of the two men, I was able to tell they were speaking of me. Something had happened which was likely to spoil my first Mardi Gras. It seems the old man was saying (in effect), "The children have been gone for an hour - and won't be home before dark. I have no way of finding them, otherwise he could have gone with them."

And they continued to talk more about the children and their joy in masking until I began to understand that even at this early hour the children, whoever they might be, were masking and mingling with others in the streets and that I was left behind. There was some talk of my uncle taking me to see the parades, but the old man said "No." The boy must mask and he must see the thing in the way it should be seen. Every child should have that pleasure once at least. He himself had masked in his childhood. It meant everything. Let's think. We'll work something out. They continue to talk while I wandered around the courtyard.

Suddenly, the old man shouted "I got it." And he picked up a small hand bell from the table and rang it several times. The old woman who had been mopping the passageway appeared. "Tell Ro'-Bear (Robert) to come at once." The old woman left and soon Robert appeared, a young Negro between twenty-five and thirty years old. The old man and Robert had a brief conversation in French. I gathered that they were talking of me. My uncle explained that Robert would take me where I could see the maskers and the parades. He would have charge of me for the day. A costume would be provided for me.

Robert disappeared for a while and then returned wearing a hat and coat. My uncle then lectured Robert: he was never to let go of my hand in the crowds, he was to see that I got a costume that we liked, and he was to see that I had something to eat at intervals. And last came the instruction which had to do with our return after the night parade. He then gave Robert five dollars - which seemed like a fortune to me - and we were ready to go.

As we turned to go, I heard my uncle ask if Robert could be trusted, and I heard the old man say, "But of course! Ro'-Bear has been with me for years, since he was a child in fact. It was I who named him for the opera Meyesbeer," 'Ro'-Bear le Diable'!"

Soon Robert and I were walking down the passage which led to the streets, my hand held tightly in his. As the door opened, I saw, in the street a group of children dressed in gay colored costumes and wearing masks. They came running by shouting with tiny bells worn as ornaments on their costumes. All shouting "Mardi Gras! Mardi Gras." Robert looked down at me with a big smile and said, "We goin tuh have us a good time."

We went through narrow streets. The shop keepers ran to their doors to shout greetings. We went past second hand furniture stores where rocking chairs seemed at home on the sidewalk. I lingered before a store where parrots screamed and alligators and snakes lived in cages side by side.

In front of the French Opera House at Bourbon and Toulouse Streets, men were carrying gilded statues up the stairs and a group of masks stood watching, making comments upon the mysterious glittering figures as they disappeared into the doorways. I wanted to linger around some of these wonders, but Robert was intent on pressing forward. Soon we turned into a little shop which seemed quite dark, but when my eyes had accustomed themselves to the dimness, I was dazed by the many new delights. It was a costume shop.

There were two rooms opening one into the other by sliding doors. In the first room were counter and shelves, with high-piled green boxes. Masks of all descriptions were strung across the room, models for display, countless costumes, hats, skulls, silly fat girls, etc.

In the second room, a woman in black sewed like mad on a sewing machine while women ran about waiting on customers. Two nuns - the same two that I had met in the street - were bargaining for the rental of a red devil costume. I heard one of the nuns say, "Ah, Madame, but you should allow us a little off the regular price . . . It's for the Church, you know!" I thought nothing of it then, but to this day the renting of that red devil costume by the nuns has remained an unsolved mystery in my mind.

At last it was our turn to be served. Robert told the woman in charge to fit me with a red devil costume. Soon I was being forced into a sort of red union suit over all my clothes. There was a hood from which two horns projected and there was a grinning devil mask. In about a minute it was done and rolled into a bundle, but Robert wasn't finished yet. He began explaining that a second costume was needed for his employer, "This child's brother." This naturally surprised me because I had no brother, but I remained silent and waited while Robert looked at this and that and finally selected some red silk tights and a few other fittings for "my brother." At last he was finished and we departed from the store with two bundles.

"Where are we going now?", I wanted to know. Robert explained that we must go to his room nearby so that we could put on our costumes. In a few minutes we were at the room and getting into the costumes. Soon two red devils emerged from the room into the street. By the time we reached Royal Street the sidewalks were full of Maskers. Our costumes, perfectly fitted so that no part if our skin was visible, no one could tell whether we were white, black, Chinese or anything else. We merged into the crowd. All going the same way, children of all sizes and ages were everywhere. Men and women hidden under some conical disguise on their way to join the merrymakers on Canal Street. A band could be heard playing in the distance.

Here amidst a great deal of ceremony, embarking would take place and the start of the Zulu parade, an all day affair, twisting and winding its way through the city drinking many toasts and eating lots of red beans and rice.

Rex, King of the Carnival, toasting his queen is a ceremony I didn't understand then and we still don't understand. But it remains one of the highlights of the Carnival Season. All I can remember is that Rex, on his high throne, sitting opposite his queen and then from somewhere came a man with a step ladder, which was set up in the street. The man ran up the ladder carrying a tray with a white napkin over it. He presented the tray to the king. Suddenly a bottle was opened with a loud pop and champagne poured out into thin wine glasses. Rex was toasting his queen. I am sure there is a story of why this was done and how old this custom is. The ceremony was soon over, the ladder was removed and Rex, on his throne, was drawn slowly down the street.

It is simply impossible to recount all of the sights, sounds and happenings of this fabulous day. As the say, "You'll have to come to the Mardi Gras" and see for yourself.

The next day, Ash Wednesday, we were back on the train headed home. We had hardly got going before Uncle Sam was fast asleep. After what seemed like a very long time, to me, he sort of stirred. I immediately asked a question that had been lurking in my subconscious mind ever since we met the old man in the courtyard who had embraced him so warmly. My question was, who was this man who seemed to live alone? Who were the children whom I still have not seen? It was obvious that Robert and the old woman were employees. Uncle Sam's answer to my question was, a sleepy "We'll talk about that later."

Eight years later my questions were answered, but not by Uncle Sam, but by one of my great aunts, Lou Gardner, who was Uncle Sam's half sister. Aunt Lou enjoyed "sharing secrets" with me because I was "a good secret keeper".

The old man's name was Antoine Richard. He was Uncle Sam's half brother. They had the same Mulatto mother. Sam's father was black making him a Griffe. Antoine's father was white making him a Quadroon. Antoine (as they say) was a crossover, i.e., left home, severed all ties with family, moved to New Orleans, passed for white and married a well-to-do white girl. The children were Antoine's teenage grandchildren, his daughter's two boys and a girl who always began Mardi Gras Day from Grandpa's house.

My first visit to New Orleans (noted elsewhere in this book) was on a Mardi Gras Day - which happened to be my birth date. I was around six or seven years old then.

When I was eleven years old I went to live in New Orleans with my mother's sister, Aunt Mamie and her husband Charley

Johnson. Most everyone called him "Creep" (affectionately). On my arrival in the big city I was immediately mesmerized by the crowds, hustle and bustle, street vendors hollering out their wares, I got watermelon lady, red to the rind just one dime, I got okra, cucumbers, collard greens and big fat rabbits lady, "There was also the ubiquitous pan handler without glasses, trying to supplement their street income at the dice, poker and Monte games at the Astoria and Pelican Clubs on Rampart Street.

While the nation was in the grips of a devastating depression, there seemed to be romance, excitement and a carnival-like atmosphere existing in New Orleans most of the time - except during the Lenten season which begins at 12:01 a.m. on Ash Wednesday and ending on Easter Sunday.

This book is an informal (but not in depth) account of New Orleans when it was known as the wickedest city in the world. The main character is the City itself. A city of intrigue, festivities, historical significance and peopled with colorful legendary characters such as Marie LaVeau Voodoo queen, George Deval gambler, Basin Street Ladies, Bordello Madames, and quadroon girls all collectively providing the heartbeat of America's Most Interesting City".

Articles, and news stories on New Orleans consulted for this book include the following.

1. The publications of the Louisiana Historical Society
2. The Colonial Archives of Louisiana
3. "New Orleans, The Place and the People by Grace King
4. "New Orleans, As it was," by Henry C. Castellanos
5. "Strange True Stories of Louisiana", by Grace King
6. Standard History in Old New Orleans" compiled by Edward Righton
7. Social Life in Old New Orleans" by Eliza Ripley
8. Files on newspapers viz; "The Times Picayune", "The New Orleans Item", Various old letters, diaries, records and legal documents cited in the text.
9. "Fabulous New Orleans", by Lyle Saxon
10. The French Quarter", by Herbert Asbury
11. Several tabloids of the times VIZ; "Sunday Sun:,

"Mascot", and the "Blue Book" published sensational accounts of crime and scandal devoting considerable space to the activities, of the red-light district and exposing corruption.

A number of senior natives made contributions (from memory) to this book in terms of what they were told about certain incidents by parents and grandparents. This information did not always agree with the tabloids.

Many writers have tried their pens on this sinful old City but caught only a few of her many aspects. In the opinion of this writer, one man alone has been able to come close to capturing the entire life of the city. He was equally at home in the uptown, the downtown, back-of-town and the front-of-town sections. His friends included Creoles, the Boston Club gang and the Saratoga Street Strumpets. He understood and loved them all and they all loved him. In his last days when he was in the hospital, friends kept trying to encourage him by telling him he would recover and go home. He knew better. "Stop worrying about me" he kept saying "I've had a wonderful time." Lyle Saxon died on April 9th 1949 at age 54. A newspaper reporter commented, "The heart of New Orleans stopped beating last night." Knowing Lyle for the first thirty years of my life and the last thirty of his inspired me to never tire of exploring every nook and corner of the old City, by street car and walking from West End to the Mississippi River, and from the industrial canal to Tulane University. And in the process, enjoying the diversity of people, customs, cultures and acquiring basic knowledge about sections like the Garden District, French Quarter, Basin Street, Speakeasies, Irish Channel, etc. I also learned that strangers to some of these sections were not welcomed after dark, a fact that most natives and cab drivers were aware of. Like most young minds I was curious and not immune to emulating the trends of the day. It was the late 20's and 30's. The time of John Dillinger, Bonnie Parker and Clyde Barrow, Pretty Boy Floyd, Machine Gun Kelly, Al Capone, Legs Diamond, Story Ville, Red-Light District, Pimps, Strumpets, Voodooism, Corrupt Politicians, Bootleg Whiskey and Gamblers. Looking back now (1997), I can fully appreciate how extremely blessed I was and how very fortunate I was to have had Aunt Mamie and Creep in my corner. They recognized early, the necessity of providing an adjustable leash for me, which was much too short, I thought.

To write a book about New Orleans in which one of it's most celebrated attractions (food) is excluded is tantamount to making Creole gumbo and leaving out the shrimp. The basis for my decision not to include food I shall try to explain to my contemporary critics:

There are, literally hundreds of fine food establishments scattered throughout New Orleans. To do justice to them all would be beyond the scope of this book. Many, naturally, would have to be omitted thereby creating a dilemma of no small proportion. Excellent guide books, complete with detail listing and ratings are available on Royal and Bourbon Streets, within a block or so of Canal Street in the heart of the French Quarter.

Most visitors to New Orleans already know, heard or believe that the food is excellent. All they want to know is where to go and get it.

Although I am a native New Orleanian, researching the many characters, whom I thought I knew fairly well, revealed some very interesting facts, sometimes shocking especially among the Basin Street Ladies, the Quadroon girls, and ghastly inhuman tortures administered by men,for instance, try to visualize, if you can, a man physically unable to do work assigned him, being punished in this way: He was stripped naked, whipped until unconscious, one eye was put out from the butt of the whip. This kind of cruelty was typical during the early history of New Orleans and Louisiana. No, "The Big Easy" as New Orleans is sometime referred to, today wasn't always easy. But yet between 1825 and 1860 the City enjoyed it's most prosperous days. Sugar cane and cotton planters were abounding in wealth. The shipping port was busy, immigrants arriving daily, new building and construction going up everywhere. Gambling and the red light district thrived. Nevertheless, the period also included the miseries of yellow fever and other plagues which seemed to always be lurking in shadows. Hurricanes and floods were constant threats. Slavery, the backbone of the economy, always there, a source of sorrow and trouble for everyone. The end of the Civil War, brought new problems - the abolition of slavery and struggles of reconstructions. New Orleans' history from then until now has been not unlike most other sections of the South. But it remains America's Most Interesting City.

Acknowledgments

I would like to extend my gratitude and thanks to the many individuals with whom I had personal contact, viz; newspaper writers, library workers, historians, scholars, and just plain old timers who remembered when Franklin Street was known as Bolivar Street, and Gravier Street was part of the red light district, and Louis Armstrong played baseball in the old Illinois Central Ball Park, near the Union Train Station.

A special thanks to, two brothers, William and Sam Casimir, with whom I grew up on Galvez and Perdido Streets. Both became members of the Fats Pichon band of the 1930's. The memories of William and Sam were a key factor in helping me to avoid the use of Pseudonyms.

I am deeply indebted to Mrs. Ruth Kennedy, New Orleans Public School Librarian, Ms. Sally Stassi and Mr. John McGill of the Historic New Orleans Collection for their valuable help with the research for the illustrations. Finally, I wish to express my deep appreciation to my wife, Leota, for her patience and kindness during many unproductive periods in writing this book. I am duly grateful for the co-operation of everybody concerned.

Chapter I

New Orleans

In the early days when New Orleans first became a part of the United States, the American section above Canal Street was the site of the most sordid and vicious of the underworld districts. The more legitimate activities of the town were found in the Vieux Carre. In spite of the Spanish characteristics, it was still more French in spirit and custom. Coffee houses cabarets and bordellos also gambling houses and eating places were plentiful. The eating places alone were destined to spread the fame of New Orleans throughout the world. When a family went out for the evening, it was quite a spectacle to see making their way slowly through the muddy streets. First came the slaves with lanterns, shoes, silk stockings and other articles of dress which were to be worn when the destination had been reached. Finally, the members of the family in boats and raincoats, each gentleman carrying his own personal lantern. Despite the discomforts, the fancy dress balls were well attended nightly, until Lent put an end to the years' festivities.

Throughout the first decade of the American Occupation, the fashionable balls and masquerades continued to be held in a wooden building on Conti (later Charters) Street near Dumaine Street. Inside the building, along the side of a hall, were boxes where the mothers and chaperons of the Creole Belles and the young girls (who were permitted to watch but not dance) sat. Below the boxes were rows of seats where the Creole Belles would rest between dances.

Behind these seats running the full length of the building, about three feet wide, the Creole Gentlemen awaited their turn to dance. They outnumbered the Belles by at last three to one, a fact that would sometimes lead to unpleasant incidents. Each young man wore a French sword (if he was properly attired), a popular weapon of the period. Quarrels sometimes arose

1

between these young hot-blooded men over what would be considered trivial today (accidentally stepping on someone's foot, brushing against another or dancing with a young lady without getting consent from her "Protector"). These and many other trivial matters were sufficient cause for a duel. Arrangements would be quickly made and the men and their seconds quietly left the ballroom to settle the matter in a selected spot behind the building. Honor was satisfied with the first blood drawn. The victor returned to the ballroom, while the wounded (or dead) were taken care of by his second.

The Old St. Louis Cemetery is located two blocks east of Bienville, between Dirbigny and Roman Streets. The author's great-great-Aunt Mezau, a former slave, lived at the Bienville Street address for many years, until she died in the early 1930's. She is buried in the Old Cemetery. There are many marble slabs of young Creole men, each testifying that he "fell in a duel." It's quite reasonable to conclude that perhaps he lies there because of his attention to a Quadroon girl whose official "Protector" objected to his flirtations. The Quadroon balls were the most celebrated of all the entertainment of early New Orleans. According to Grace King, a well-known native writer of the period, the pure-blooded African was never called colored, but always Negro. The colored people were a class apart; separate from and superior to the Negro. They were superior if but one drop of white blood flowed in their veins. The caste seems to have existed from the first introduction of slaves in the Colony. Lyle Saxon, a highly regarded New Orleans writer, ventured the opinion that, when there were no white women in the Colony numerous Mulatto children were born to Negro slave women.

In many instances the father set these women free and since under the law, children always shared the conditions of their mother, they became free also and so began an increase in number of gens de couleur libres (free Colored people). As Grace Kings says, "they formed a part of the population at a very early date in the history of Louisiana, as far back as six years after its founding of New Orleans." They were, by law, forbidden to marry either their own slaves or slaves owned by white men.

After the American occupation, these free men and women were designated in the newspapers and legal documents simply by the initials F.M.C. and F.W.C. They were few in numbers until after the Civil War, when, theoretically at least, all Negroes became free. From the beginning of their existence in Louisiana, the free people of color maintained a society of their own, in which class lines were as rigidly drawn as among the whites. The Griffe looked down on the pure-blooded Negroes, the Mulatto regarded the Griffe with scorn, the Quadroon looked down on the Mulatto, while the Octoroon refused to socialize with any of the others. The majority of all these free men and women of color were law-abiding and very industrious. "By 1830", wrote Charles Gayarre, a historian, "many of these people had become wealthy enough to own cotton and sugar plantations and numerous slaves. They educated their children in France where some chose to remain having attained distinction in science and literature. Those who chose to return to New Orleans became musicians, merchants, money and real estate brokers. Some became mechanics, barbers, tailors, carpenters and brick masons."

The free Negro shouldered the responsibility of citizenship with few privileges. In spite of his wealth and education he was usually denied the vote. John W. Blassingame, writer, in his book *The Negro in Antebellum New Orleans*, observed that while he (the Negro) was denied the privileges of Antebellum society, he was required to protect that same society by serving as guardsmen in New Orleans and on slave patrols to keep peace. Andrew Jackson did not hesitate in calling upon the free Negroes to defend a city which denied them their manhood. New Orleans was a very puzzling city to the visitors. There was no residential segregation, sometimes even sharing rooming houses. They danced, gambled and drank together in many of the bars and restaurants in spite of laws against such activities. The brothels were integrated even the staff and customers. Black men were known to marry white women without much public concern. A Negro hair dresser remembers a black man who married a "white beauty" from Virginia in New Orleans. Everyone knew he was a Mulatto, but because of his wealth and his father, nothing was

3

said. There were many more, e.g., a white Baton Rouge school teacher, Alice C. Riley said, a friend of hers, Min Coulin, who was "purely white", married a Mulatto. He was one of the wealthiest men on the Bayou Teche, about six miles southwest of New Orleans and happens to be the birthplace of the Author. It was not uncommon to see white women claiming to be Negroes to marry men of their choice.

Mulatto women seldom formed any kind of alliance with black males. Actually, by law, the light-skin free Negro was not allowed to mingle with the dark-skinned slave. Social status was directly related to color. The Negro's status grew in direct proportion to the whiteness of his skin. The visitor and stranger to New Orleans was mystified and confused by the many gradations of color. For convenience the word mulatto was commonly applied to all of them. The following definitions were generally accepted by the natives:

The child of a white and Negro a Mulatto
The child of a white and Mulattoa Quadroon
The child of a white and Quadroon-an Octoroon
The child of a Mlatto and Quadroon-a Tierceron
The child of a Negro and Mulatto-a Griffe
The child of a Mulatto and Griffe-a Marabon
The child of a Negro and Griffe-a Sacatren

One visitor noted, "You may not be able to distinguish one from the other, but you can be certain they all exist in New Orleans." Commenting on the women, an English woman traveler said they were "probable as beautiful and accomplished a set of women as can be found." Another observer called them "gentle and pleasant." The most impressed of all was a German nobleman. To him the women were "the most beautiful in the world."

The white male had an insatiable desire for sexual relations with Negro women; so much so that something special had to come into being in order to satisfy that desire. Sex relations with Negro women were common and accepted as the privilege of the white man. It was not unusual for a wealthy white man to purchase a beautiful Negro woman for his personal use. The best known arrangement for the white man to carry on his liaison with the Negro woman was known as the placage.

Usually a placage would begin at a Quadroon ball. When a white gentleman found a Negro girl whom he desired, he proceeded to court her the same as he would the other girls to whom he would probably marry some day. These beautiful Quadroons were very popular and most cases had to choose from among several white beaux. Following a period of courtship the suitor would enter an agreement with the girl's parents whereby he would agree to purchase her a house and provide a certain amount of money for each of the children that might result from the union.

Some writers and others viewed the placage as a system of prostitution. If this be so then common law marriage where large numbers of white and Negro couples live together without being married would have to be defined.

Chapter II

Voodoo

Frequently, since the first publishing of <u>Cooking with St. Claire</u>, my first book, readers have asked me questions about Voodooism in Louisiana. Was it true or fictional? Does it still exist?

Having spent my early years growing up in New Orleans, Jeanerette and Albania Plantation, I can say Voodooism definitely did exist. I suspect it still exists today, although on a much smaller scale.

My great-Aunt Lena Lovette, who operated the boarding house at Albania Plantation during the latter part of the 1800s, was a storehouse of information on Voodooism according to my father St. Clair deClouet. He lived with her from the time his parents died (he was about seven years old) until she turned the operation of the boarding house over to him after a 15 year apprenticeship and moved to New Orleans where she died and is buried in the old St. Louis Cemetery in Basin St. - the final resting place of Marie Laveau.

During those 15 years of living and working with Aunt Lena, my father said she told him many Voodoo stories which he, in turn, enjoyed telling his children. According to Aunt Lena, as told by my father, by the end of the 19th century Voodooism was well entrenched in Louisiana as a secret society throughout both the slave and free Negro populations.

A message could be sent from one end of the slave quarters to another in relatively short time without one white person being aware of it. A Negro cook in a kitchen would sing some Creole song while rattling pots and pans. A song which sounded innocent enough to any white listener, but at the end of the verse she would sing a few words intended as a message. Another Negro would then go outside to attend to her duties. She would sing the same song and her voice would be heard by servants in the house next door. In this way, by means of song news, an impending meeting would be announced. On the appointed night, men and women would slip from their beds before midnight to assemble for their Voodoo ceremonies.

The fear inspired by the Voodoo leaders was so strong that members of the sect could be induced to commit almost any crime. Now the questions, "Did the Voodoo believers possess supernatural powers?", always drew, "No comment." from my father as an answer, although I am quite certain he did not approve of the practice of Voodooism, nor did he take those who did seriously. It did seem, however, quite clear that the practitioners possessed a knowledge of drugs and poisons and that their white masters were powerless before them. It was believed that many masters were poisoned by their slaves and in many instances no motives could be proven. The Voodoo people were quick to have their sect believe certain deaths or misfortunes were the results of powers they brought to bear.

There are many stories of Voodoo doctors and queens who reigned before Marie Laveau, but none gaining the fame and lasting power of the beautiful Mulatto. As one story goes:

A police captain in 1855 raided the house of the Voodoo doctor, Don Pedro. He found about 12 white women and as many Negro men essentially naked all engaged in amusing themselves under the direction of the doctor. Although Don Pedro protested they were being treated for rheumatism, they were all arrested and fined. Next day the husband of one of the women committed suicide.

Dr. John appeared to be the first Voodoo doctor of record in New Orleans. One of his clients, the famous beautiful Mulatto slave Pauline, was the first Negro to be executed after the American occupation of New Orleans. She also won the distinction of being the first person to be hanged in the Parish prison located then behind Congo Square in 1832. This prison was demolished in 1895. A new one was erected at Tulane and Broad Streets.

Pauline secured the help of Dr. John in becoming the mistress of her master, Peter Redeck. According to the records and newspapers, Peter Redeck went to St. Louis on business sometime in December of 1844. In January of 1845, the Mayor,

Edgar Montegut, was notified anonymously that a white woman was being kept prisoner in her home at 52 Bayou Road. On the 14th of January the mayor and police officers went to the Bayou Road address which was the home of Peter Redeck. They found Mrs. Redeck and hr three children ranging in ages from 2 through 7 confined in a cabinet.

It appears the slave Pauline had taken possession of the house immediately after Redeck left for St. Louis. Mrs. Redeck told the authorities that she and her children had been kept prisoners in their house for six weeks during which time they were beaten and starved. She was also taunted with remarks about her husband's unfaithfulness.

Pauline was tried, found guilty and sentenced to death. The execution was postponed to March 28, 1846 because she was found to be pregnant. The disposition of Pauline's pregnancy remains moot. Probing research has failed to produce a clue. Dressed in a long white robe and white cap her arms bound, she was hanged in the courtyard of the Parish Prison.

In any discussion of Voodooism, the name of Marie Laveau must be mentioned. She was considered the Queen of Voodoo and the subject of many stories of wonder in New Orleans. According to records in the Archives of the St. Louis Cathedral in New Orleans under the signature of the famous Pere Antoine, there is registered the marriage of Jacques Paris and Marie Laveau on August 4, 1819. Both were free Negroes. Jacques died in 1826 and shortly thereafter his widow entered into a relationship with a Christope Glopion. Several children were born to them, one of which was named Marie. Marie, being a natural daughter, took her mother's maiden name Laveau. She was born on February 2, 1827. I could find nothing of her childhood, but as a young woman, I found she was known to the police as a black magic worker. It was then that she became known officially as the Voodoo Queen. Even today, when I visit New Orleans, I still hear mothers use her name to frighten naughty children. "You better be good or Marie Laveau will get you!"

Here's what Henri Castillanos, in his book New Orleans As It Was, has to say about Marie Laveau:

In her youth she was a woman of fine physique. Introducing herself into families as a hairdresser, she would assist in the clandestine correspondence of sweethearts and aid youthful lovers. She was an essentially bad woman. Though Queen of the "voudous", she exercised the ritual of the original creed so as to make it conform to the worship of the Virgin and of other Saints. To idolatry she added blasphemy. She was the first to popularize "voudouism" in New Orleans, inviting members of the press, of the sporting fraternity and others to the yearly festivals held on St. John's Eve (June 24th) at some spot not far from the Bayou which bears that name. She also dealt in charms against malefices and pretended to cure ailments produced by "gris-gris" (little red bags containing powdered brick, yellow ochre and cayenne pepper, which were supposed to cause untold injury to the recipient) and other criminal devices.

There are many other stories told of her. In an article by G. William Nott, which appeared in the New Orleans "Times-Picayune", is found the following:

It will not be amiss to relate the story of an octogenarian mammy who says that Marie Laveau was not a wicked woman, but much maligned by her enemies, and that what powers she had were used for the good of others as the following tale will prove. A certain wealthy young man in New Orleans, many years ago, had been arrested in connection with a crime and though his companions were in reality the guilty ones, blame was laid upon his shoulders. The grief-stricken father immediately sought Marie Laveau, explained to her the circumstances of the case, and offered her a handsome reward if she would obtain his son's release. When the day set for the trial came around, the wily "voodoo", after placing three Guinea peppers in her mouth, entered the St. Louis Cathedral, knelt at the altar rail and was seen to remain in this posture for some time. Leaving the church, she gained admittance to the Cabildo where the trial was held and depositing three of the peppers under the judge's bench, lingered to await developments. After a lengthy deliberation, though the evidence seemed unfavorable to the prisoner, the jury finally made its report and the judge was heard to pronounce the words, "Not Guilty." The joy of the anxious father may well be imagined. His first act was to find Marie Laveau and as a recompense for her miraculous intervention gave her the deed to a small cottage. The cottage situated on St. Anne between Rampart and Burgundy Streets remained her home to the time of her death. As a further proof of her charity, an incident is related, which though exhibiting the above name virtue, shows traces of cunning as well. A young man came to her door on one occasion, ragged and destitute, begging for alms. As she herself was short on funds, she could give him nothing, but summoning her nimble wits, she evolved a scheme that promptly bore fruit. Laying the man on a couch in her front room and covering him with a sheet, she proceeded to light a candle which she placed at his head and feet. This done, she stationed herself on the door steps, tin cup in hand, begging the money with which to defray the poor deceased man's funeral. The success of the plan was almost instantaneous (she well knew the Negroes' love for wakes), and cup overflowing with coins she returned indoors to share the profits with the speedily resurrected "corpse". Another quaint occurrence in the same house is recounted by an eyewitness: One of Marie Laveau's protegees had passed away, this time in reality, and the interment was to take place from her "front parlor". Came the hour for the funeral and as soon as the coffin had been borne away, followed by the Queen and motley assemblage, three Negro ladies, one with broom, the others with buckets and a Negro man rushed out of the house, the former like some ancient Furies, and scoured with savage energy the brick banquette, removing every trace of the mourners' footprints.

An then, a little later in the same article, Mr. Nott has this to say:

Again a narrative of Marie Laveau's strange career. In 1884, a violent hurricane passed over the city. She was then living in a shanty on Lake Pontchartrain. The force of the wind was so great that her cabin was wrenched from its foundations and hurled into the angry waters. Obliged to seek shelter on the roof, there she remained for several hours, discouraging the attempts of her would- be rescuers and telling them, "Mo oule mourri dan lac la" (I want to die in that lake). However, she was finally prevailed upon to accept the assistance offered and none to soon, for the cabin she was so loath to leave was completely shattered by the waves a few moments later. To this day, the superstitious Darkies will tell you that not until Marie was safe ashore did the fury of the storm abate.

It was previously mentioned that the black priestess dealt in "gris-gris". To the casual reader this word will mean little or nothing, but to an impressionable Negro, it is one to be conjured with. If by chance a dusky house-keeper, upon opening her front blinds found a "gris-gris" deposited on the door sill, loud were her vociferations. Immediately would she repair to Marie Laveau, wailing in the streets, "appe voudou moin, appe voudou moin" (I have been voudoued). Terror-stricken and almost speechless, she would inform the black Queen of the dire calamity that had befallen her and implore her assistance. This, Marie would immediately promise. Searching some little chest or drawer, she would find a counter "gris-gris" guaranteed to destroy the evil effects of the original, which for the modes sum of one or two dollars she would place in the hands of the grateful supplicant. Of course, there could b no doubt as to the efficacy of the second package for had she not manufactured the contents of the first as well? This latter fact, however, she deemed wise to keep to herself. An old gentleman who remembers Marie Laveau from his childhood days, will tell how she was held in dread by many of the residents below Canal Street, white as well as colored. He describes her as having a "Voltairian look", penetrating and taking in everything at a glance; an attribute quite disconcerting to the children of the neighborhood, who would listen with terror when their black nurses threatened to "give them to Marie" if they failed to obey. Whether or not the famous Marie Laveau possessed supernatural powers has long been a subject of discussion among the ignorant. More enlightened people have dismissed her as a crass imposter, though not denying for an instant the prestige she held among her own race. However, with her death, "voudouism" all but disappeared from New Orleans. The little that is practiced today assumes a harmless form; a few chicken bones placed on a door step, a black cross mark on a front board, a bright red powder sprinkled on the banquette; these are the last vestiges of the once dreaded "gris-gris".

In the old St. Louis Cemetery on Basin Street is a neat brick tomb, with the following inscription:

Famille Vve. Paries,
nee Laveau

This is all that remains to recall the former greatness of the all powerful Voudou Queen.

About fifteen years after Dr. John had retired a rich man, a slave by the name of Washington took over. Among the Negroes he was known as Dr. Yah Yah. His favorite magic cure-all was a mixture of jimpson weed, sulphur and honey, sipped from a glass which had been rubbed against a black cat with one white foot. In 1861, Dr. Yah Yah gave a bottle of his medicine to an Italian and was arrested when the Italian's physician told the police that it was a deadly poison. Dr. Yah Yah's master paid a fine of fifteen dollars and Washington was sent into the country to work as a field hand. A few years later a Dr. Jack took over. He was especially noted for effectiveness of his love charms. The best seller of these was a beef heart scented with spices and perfumes and wrapped in white crepe. It was known to never fail if left on a doorstep. In spite of its cost, $20.00, it was in great demand.

Above Dr. Jack's bed at his home on Treme Street, hung a charmed beef heart. He often told his customers that he could not die until it fell to the floor. When he died on June 10, 1869, his wife told the police that the beef heart had fallen three days before and that Dr. Jack had immediately "sickened".

The Voodoo queens and doctors seem to have been on equal footings so far as the practice of the sorcery was concerned, but in all matters affecting the actual worship of the cult, the Queen possessed supreme authority. She fixed the time and place of every voodoo meeting held in New Orleans during the course of the year. One of the earliest voodoo queens was a quadroon named Sanite' De'de' who dominated voodooism in New Orleans for more than ten years after Louisiana had become a part of the United States of America. She was a free woman from Santo Domingo. In her time the meetings of the voodoos were held in the Old Dumaine Street brickyard. The abandoned slave cabins were used as dressing rooms. The actual ceremonies and dances were held in the brick shed. One of the few white persons ever to witness a voodoo meeting in this place was a fifteen-year-old New Orleans boy. On a night in 1825, he was taken to the brickyard by a slave woman belonging to his father. Many years later, the boy had become a wealthy planter in Plaquemine Parish. This is his description of the experience:

"An entrance door was opened at the call of De'de' and I witnessed a scene which, old as I am, no passing of years can ever dim. The first thing that struck me as we entered was a built-up square of bricks at the upper and lower ends of the shed on each of which was burning a fierce fire casting a lurid light over the scene. Along the four sides of the parallelogram of the building were sconces with lighted dips placed at equal distances, which barely added to the darling light of the two pyres... Each man and woman had a white kerchief tied around the forehead, through the heads of the latter were covered by the traditional Madras handkerchief, with its five, nay, its seven artistic points upturned to Heaven. In a little while the company, some sixty in all, had assembled. There were males and females, old and young, Negro men and women - handsome Mulatresses and Quadroons, with them half a dozen white men and two white women... Near where I stood was an oblong table about eight feet in length and four in width. On its right end stood a black cat, and on its left a white one. I thought them alive and, having a certain fondness for cats, stretched out my hand to stroke the nearest. The touch, that most philosophical of all senses, soon satisfied me that they were fine specimens of Negro taxidermy. Admirably stuffed, they were too. In the center of the table there was a cypress sapling, some four feet in height, planted in the center of a firkin or keg. Immediately behind the cypress and towering above it was a black doll with a dress variegated by cabalistic signs and emblems, and a necklace of the vertebrae of snakes around her neck from which dipenden an alligator's fang encased in silver. At the side of this table I recognized an old Negro, the name of Zozo, well known in New Orleans as a vender of palmetto and sassafras roots; in fact he had a whole pharmacopoeia of samples and herbs, some salutary, but others said to be fatal. He seemed to be the conypheus of these unhallowed rites for the signal of the beginning of the work came from him. He was astride of a cylinder made of thin cypress staves hooped with brass and headed by a sheepskin. With two sticks he droned away a monotonous ra-tat-ta, ra-ra-ta-ta, while on his left sat a Negro on a low stool, who with two sheep shank bones, and a Negro woman, with the leg bones of a buzzard or turkey, beat an accompaniment on the sides of the cylinder. It was a queer second to this satanic discord. Some two feet from those arch-musicians squatted a young Negro vigorously twirling a long calabash. It was made of one of our Louisiana gourds a foot and a half long and filled with pebbles.

At a given signal the four initiates formed a crescent before De'de', who was evidently the high priestess or voudou queen. She made cabalistic signs over them and sprinkled them with some liquid from a calabash in her hand, muttering under her breath. She raised her hand and Zozo dismounted from his cylinder and from some hidden receptacle in or behind the black doll, drew an immense snake, which he brandished wildly aloft...He talked and whispered to it. At every word the reptile, with undulating body and lambent tongue, seemed to acknowledge the dominion asserted over it. In the meantime, with arms crossed and reverent eyes, the initiates had now formed a crescent around Zozo. He now compelled the snake to stand upright for about ten inches of its body...In that position Zozo passed the snake over the heads and around the neck of the initiates, repeating at each pass the words which constitute the name of this African sect, "Voudou Magnian". Hardly was this last ceremony over when a long, deep howl of exultation broke from every part of the shed. Zozo back to his tam-tam, his accompanies right and left and the gourd musician with his rattle. A banjo player, too, sprang up and pandemonium was unloosed. In the twinkling of an eye on little brick foundations boards were laid for a supper table...No benches, no seats of any kind. Some squatted on their haunches, others reclined, like the

Romans.

After the meal came a general call for the dance. No dance of the witches in the Hartzberg ever came close to it. Up sprang a magnificent specimen of human flesh - Ajona, a lithe, tall, black woman with a body waving and undulating like Zozo's snake. She tore the white handkerchief from her forehead. This was a signal for everyone to join the dance. What seemed like a chorus of Dante's hell had entered into the assembly. The orgies were becoming frightful. I had grown sick from heat and a sudden harrow took possession of me. I was out of the shed in nothing flat - I found the gate open and I was in the street and making it for home. If I ever have realized a sense of the real visible presence of the devil, it was that night among his voudou worshipers."

As we already know Sanite De'de' was succeeded by Marie Laveau. The next voodoo queen was Malvina Latour who received the scepter from the aged, trembling hands of Marie Laveau...Malvina was a Mulatto, cafe' au Lait in color whose brother became a member of the "black and tan" legislature which governed Louisiana for several years during reconstruction times. She was about thirty years old when she took over the reins from Marie Laveau, and is said to have been very handsome with a fine, fully developed figure. While her magical powers appear to have been inferior to Marie Laveau's, one of her exploits certainly equaled anything her predecessor had done. Soon after her ascension to the throne, a Reverend Mr. Turner, who was chaplain of the Louisiana Legislature, became ill of a strange sickness which caused the symptoms delirium, tremors, although he was a teetotaler. Various doctors failed to help him. Mr. Turner concluded he was a victim of a voodoo charm.

Upon the advice of Malvina Latour's brother, he sought the aid of the Voodoo queen. She directed that he be carried into a Negro church and laid upon a plain board table and that the general public be invited to watch her drive out the evil spirit which possessed the preacher. At the appointed time, the Voodoo queen began her work in the presence of a large crowd, which included Lieutenant Governor Oscar J. Dunn, a Negro.

She first manipulated the preacher's hand and then she rubbed his chest with a pungent oil, meanwhile chanting a voodoo exorcism. This concluded, she stepped back, where upon the preacher moved violently, his mouth opened and out popped a black mouse, which made a few squeaks, leaped to the floor and ran across the room disappearing into a knothole. The preacher was cured.

Malvina Latour made many changes in the ritual; she cast out the Catholic features, abolished the snakes. But the yearly celebration continued to be as they had been in Marie Laveau's time: a public spectacle, whites were admitted upon invitation on presentation of a police pass. A journalist escorted by Chief of Police Zach Bachemin attended a meeting of Voodoo on St. John's Eve in 1884 and described it in part, for an old New Orleans Guide Book. The rites were observed in a house on the shore of Lake Pontchartrain about three-fourths of a mile below Milnebury. The journalist was disappointed, it was not what he had expected. His only comment was : "The only person enjoying the aristocratic privilege of a chair was a bright cafe' au lait woman of about forty-eight, who sat in one corner of the room looking with an air of dignity. Beside her, two old Negro women continuously whispered to her. She said little. She was extremely handsome. On inquiry it was learned that her name was Malvina Latour, and that she was the queen."

Malvina Latour was the queen of Voodooism in New Orleans for almost twenty years, but she didn't have the power or compelling power of Marie Laveau. As a consequence, the organization of the cult began to disintegrate. Voodoo doctors began to assume the duties and privileges of priests. They formed groups over which they presided at ceremonies which usually involved sexual orgies. One of their so called doctors whose name was James Alexander from Mississippi, a tall slim Mulatto who boasted that he had been born "with a caul and a gift from God in his hands". Doctor Alexander had an office on Orleans Street and associated with him were Doctor Sal otherwise known as Solomon Hastings and a Negro woman, Annie Gould who lived on Monroe Street near Royal and sold voodoo charms by mail. When the police finally raided her

17

home, in 1894, they found a score of human and dog skulls, countless jars filled with dried snakes, lizards, frogs and horned toads. Doctor Alexander's main confederate in taking care of the gullible, however, was a white woman, Lou Jackson, who operated an assignation house on Roman Street. He used her premises for the orgies which were staged frequently under his direction in the name of Voodoo. If additional women were required, Lou Jackson provided them. Neighbors often complained of the noise at these gatherings. Finally on May 28, 1889, Captain Donnelly and eight policemen of the Fifth Precinct found their way into the house. In a large upstairs room they found ten Negro men, half naked, lying on the floor while fifteen white women, similarly undressed, sat on chairs arranged in a circle about them. In the center of the group was Dr. Alexander, prancing and shouting, clad simply in a blue sash and a pair of knee-length drawers made of silk netting, with a large mesh. The "Time-Democrat" said this: "The police were not prepared for so immoral a show, and for a few minutes could only look on in listless apathy. Recovering their self-possession, the officers quickly set about to perform their duty, and in the twinkling the men and women were carted off to the station for safe keeping."

Among the prisoners were two seventeen year-old girls, one of whom was accompanied by her mother. All of the prisoners were arraigned in court next day and found guilty of disorderly conduct. Dr. Alexander and Lou Jackson were each fined twenty-five dollars, and each of the others two dollars and a half.

By the time Malvina Latour retired as Queen of the Voodoos, about 1890, the word itself had been changed to "Hoodoo" and the cult had split into a score of disorganized small groups.

Chapter III

Basin Street Ladies

New Orleans was beginning to be known as America's most interesting city. Famous for the ballrooms, cafes, coffee houses, elegant gambling halls, restaurants and Mardi Gras. Notoriously world-wide as a sin-din. Because of the wide-spread of prostitution and the tolerance with which it was regarded by the authority and the people as a whole. For many years it was the most firmly entrenched phase of underworld activity in the city. It was big business, giving employment to thousands, and many illegal dollars changing hands. Without the "girls" it is doubtful if such districts as Gallatin Street and the Franklin Street areas, described by Mr. Bison William's, a writer, as the only locality in the city where decent people do not live, could have existed.

Prostitution early on was confined to the districts frequented by lusty river men with the exception of a few "high class places", which operated with considerable immunity to the law, in Royal, Chartres, and other streets of the French Quarters. Later, around the middle 1800s when New Orleans began developing as an important seaport and cosmopolitan city, the Municipal government was corrupt and demoralized. It was during this period that prostitution began to leave the underworld section of town and establish itself in New Quarters above Canal Street. From this point it would later involve the Vieux Carre.

The authorities made feeble attempts to stop this march of harlots into the residential areas despite the complaints of property owners who were forced to leave those homes because of the boisterous brothels. By 1870 when New Orleans had a population of 190,000, bordellos of many descriptions, from the ten dollar parlor house to the fifteen cent crib, were operating wide open on such important streets as St. Charles, Basin, Royal, Canal, Poydras, Union, Burgandy, Iberville, Bienville, Rampart, Toulouse, St. Peter, Villere, Dauphine, Perdido, St. Louis,

Gasquet (now Cleveland), Common, Franklin and many others besides. Except in the outlying part of the city, there were hardly any blocks in New Orleans which did not have at least one brothel. It was common knowledge that all paid tribute to the corrupt politicians, the police and other state and city government officials. These grafters received as much as $200.00 a week from each of the large parlor houses and $20.00 from the lowly cribs. Business was exceptionally good during Mardi Gras celebrations. However, when business was slow these politicians and officials where astute enough to not only forego their weekly take but frequently advanced money to pay the running expenses of the brothels, until business improved. In addition, many of the larger parlor houses were financed and erected by city and state officials as a prime investment.

The Cop on the beat and the precinct Officers seldom shared in big money that found its way to their superiors. They had their own methods of shakedown. They demanded twenty-five cents a week from each girl of the crib and a dollar from each girl working out of the more elegant parlor houses. Payments for officials and politicians where usually made through bartenders or civilian agents. Many officials went from house to house making their own collections. The money for the Cop on the beat was usually left on the stoop on designated nights. There are still people in New Orleans (including the writer) who recall the days when little piles of quarters and dollars could be seen on the door steps of brothels (among milk bottles) by early risers. Newspaper reporters remember when policemen assigned to the red-light district came into the station house at weekly intervals with their pockets bulging with coins.

While many New Orleans streets acquired fame as places of vice during the Civil War and reconstruction periods and successfully maintained their reputation for many years thereafter; none reached the towering height of world-wide notoriety as did Basin Street. Basin Street began at Peter Street in the French Quarter, ran southward to Canal Street and continued southward to Toledony Street. Basin Street does not exist anymore, but it is still remembered in a popular blues song which describes it as "heaven on earth" and "the place where the white and black folk meet".

For almost fifty years it was the main street of the red-light district, running through the heart of New Orleans, and during the greater part of that time, after the turn of the century, it's principal business was Vice from St. Louis Street to Tulane Avenue. Luxurious pretentious and expensive brothels lined both sides of the street, said to be the best in the United States. Three-story mansions of brick and brownstone, many of them financed and built with the aid of politicians and state and city officials and filled with mahogany and black walnut woodwork and furniture, oriental rugs, silver door knobs, grand pianos, carved marble fireplaces and copies of famous paintings. A reporter for the New Orleans Times, in company with a police official, visited one of these dives of Basin Street in the late 1800s and made, in effect, these comments; entrance to the brothel, he wrote on February 7, was "through a passageway adorned with a couple of statues representing some obscure divinities of light, and in whose hands were held lighted flambeaux. Beyond this lay the drawing room, peopled with a few figures in glittering attire, and who, from their costumes and manners, might have been visitors from the Mountains of the Moon. The bizarre aspect of everything – splendor without comfort – was suggestive of death and decay. All of this together gave rise to singular reflections. But what reflections, the reporter didn't say.

Only wine and champagne were served in these palaces; the ladies wore evening gowns and could be seen in many houses, by appointment only. Between business conferences in their boudoirs with their gentlemen callers, they were entertained by strolling musicians, dancers, singers and jugglers, nightly; who went from house to house offering their performances, some of the larger brothels were staffed by as many as thirty girls, each of whom paid her Madame from thirty to fifty dollars a week for board and lodging, and as much more for laundry and incidentals. The fees paid by customers ranged from five to twenty dollars for one experience and from twenty to fifty dollars if the gentleman wished to spend the night. Breakfast was served to the all-nighter and cab fare home if necessary.

In later years Basin Street declined in tone and increased in viciousness. The rates underwent drastic reductions. Plenty of girls were available in Basin Street for a dollar. The wine was replaced by beer, the evening gowns by "shake babes" or nothing at all. No more strolling musicians.

Originally, during the early 1800s, for about twenty years, Basin Street was one of the finest residential districts in the City, with great mansions occupied by wealthy American families. But unfortunately this was the path of the prostitutes when they started their movement from Tchoupitoulas Street through Common, Canal, Perdido, Rampart, Union and other streets where bordellos were established several years before the Civil War.

The first big brothel was erected about 1866 by Kate Townsend at #40 Basin Street. According to a article of the New Orleans Time from September 22, 1870, signed "Suffering Property Holder", it was built at the expense of a high police official, a Recorder and several members of the Common Council. The article continued, "We have understood that the lady of an Alderman, who heard that her husband visited the house, resolved to see for herself. She disguised herself and entered the house, where she found nearly the whole city government, with the President of the Board of Alderman and the Mayor – we forget which - at the head table and her husband at the foot".

Of course there are no records to prove or disprove "Suffering Property Holder" statements, but most likely they were correct; for Kate Townsend was one of the most influential Madames in the history of New Orleans. Her bordello was a favorite watering hole of the politicians and city officials. Her successful move to Basin Street paved the way for others to follow. Within a few years the finest part of the street above Canal Street had lost its respectability "The Suffering Property Holder" said this in the Times.

The opening of another of those whited sepulchers on Basin Street offers a fittey opportunity of calling attention of the public, and particular the city authorities and the police, to the condition of this fine street. Between Canal and Common

Streets, almost every house is of bad repute, lighted up at night with music and revelry within, having a constant stream of men going in and out, and the late investigation into the homicide that took place in the den #40 reveals the scenes that are nightly therein enacted. To such a state has the neighborhood come that several of our most respectable citizens have had to sell their family mansions at half the price they cost to build; and have removed from the locality, and others we learn are about to follow, as they cannot permit their families longer to remain within hearing and seeing of the nightly orgies that are going on here.

A good many of the prostitutes and brothel keepers who followed Kate Townsend into Basin Street remained for many years; their names and memories of their places are still preserved in tradition of the red-light district. One enterprising beauty who called herself Minnie Haha and claimed to be a descendent of the heroine of Longfellow's poem. She had a brothel on Union Street but put a housekeeper in charge while she opened a swanky place on Basin Street near Kate Townsend's mansion. In front of the house she installed a granite hitching-block with gilded iron rings with her name chiseled upon it in large letters. The post was attended by a uniformed Negro boy wearing a red jacket with Minnie Haha embroidered on the chest in gold. For the house bags of apples were provided. When a gentleman spent the night he found in the morning, his clothing pressed, shoes shined, and a hot breakfast.

At #18 Basin Street, a few doors down from Minnie's place, Lerla Barton operated a brothel; described by the Times as "one of the most fashionable palaces of the time (1870)". According to the Times, on March 5th, "Mrs. H., wife of a well-known merchant, walked in with a new six-shooter and fired at Blanche Russell", one of the "girls", who Mrs. H. said was her husband's mistress. Fortunately, no one was hurt, the gun misfired five times, only one of the cartridges exploded. Gentle Annie Reed opened a big house at #88 Basin Street about 1868, but about a year later she moved to Customhouse Street. Kitty Johnson ran #88 for many years, she was noted for her many lovers. Two of them, Billy Walsh and J. J. Heley fought a duel on the sidewalk in front of the house in 1882, while Kitty and her staff watched from the windows. The cook, in the meantime, had been instructed to prepare a fine dinner for the victor. Walsh was killed after several shots were fired; said the States on August 2nd, "Billy Walsh was a notoriously wicked man for many years. He was a cab driver, a detective and gambler. During his turbulent life in this city he was engaged in many disreputable affrays and finally terminated his career as he lived riotously in blood".

Josephine Killeen, ran a brothel at #45 Basin Street, opposite Kate Townsend's. The big attraction there was the ten-year-old daughter of Molly William's (one of the prostitutes). Mother and child were offered jointly for fifty dollars a night. When the police said this was going a bit too far and took the little girl away, Josephine Killeen called their action an outrage; she said that the child was simply helping her Mother get along in the world.

Number 21 Basin Street was run by Hattie Hamilton, one of three women who made Basin Street history (the others were Kate Townsend and Fanny Sweet) and the mistress of Senator James D. Beares, described by the states as "one of the most flagrant and corrupt Senators under the radical regime, and whose vote for a measure was only to be obtained by him receiving a substantial reward.

Hattie Hamilton's maiden name was Peacock, said to have been the daughter of a prosperous shopkeeper in Port Richmond, New York. She was married to Samuel W. Plume, in 1855. He took her to Cuba where their one child was born (a son). When Plume learned she was on the roster of a Havana call-house, he sent her back to New York and he came to New Orleans with his son a few years later. He became a policeman. In 1864, his wife appeared in New Orleans in company of a gambler called "Colonel" Hamilton. For several years, they were seen together about town. During this time Hattie was renowned for her beauty and charm. When she began to gain notoriety for promiscuity, the "Colonel" cast her off and her husband Plume divorced her. In 1866, she entered Tilly Phillip's brothel in

Rampart Street. Early in 1869, she moved to Julia Davis' Place in Customhouse Street, one of the toughest dives in the city and in April that year was one of three harlots arrested by Plume for fighting.

Not long after this incident, Hattie's luck took a turn for the better. She met Senator Beares and must have impressed him with her beauty and skills so much so that he took her out of the Davis' Place and bought her fine clothes, a red-wheeled carriage, a pair of high-stepping horses and instilled her in style as the Madame of #21 Basin Street. She promptly staffed the place with beautiful and accomplished tenants. Under her expert management, twenty-one became one of the most popular brothels in the city. Once twenty-one was running smoothly, however, Hattie turn the day-to-day operations over to the housekeeper and began to spend much of her time at the home of Senator Beares on St. Charles Avenue, posing as his wife. It was said that they engaged in long drinking bouts, sometimes lasting for days. On May 26, 1870, after dinner the Senator and Hattie began drinking heavily, Robert Phillips, the Negro butler heard them quarreling and scuffling about the room. About dawn, the Negro heard a shot, and a few minutes later found the Senator lying on a couch dying from a bullet wound in the abdomen, while Hattie sat in a chair in a stupefied, drunken manner. On the floor between them was a pistol which disappeared during the next few hours and was never found.

Phillips notified the Senators brother, George Beares, who in turn notified the police. Hattie Hamilton was taken into custody but not formally arrested, and was released within twenty-four hours without being questioned. George Beares refused to make a charge against the woman, but he did accuse the Negro butler, and Phillips was arrested as an accessory to the murder. But when George Beares was examined on June 7, 1870 by Recorder Walsh, he said he knew nothing of the case and refused to testify. Patrick Clark a close friend of the Senator and a frequent visitor to his home swore he had never seen Phillips before he appeared in court. The Negro was released and the investigation abandoned. It was generally believed that Hattie and Phillips knew so much of the Senator's secrets, that his friend and relatives, could not afford to go further into the circumstances of the killing.

Business began to decline at #21 Basin Street. Hattie sold the place and opened up a place at #158 Customhouse Street, which was a notorious dive for ten years. Hattie died at Old Point Comfort Virginia on August 9, 1882, leaving her property to David Jackson, owner of the Gem Concert-Saloon on Royal Street. The court determined that Hattie had been his mistress since 1877. The newspaper estimated her estate at $200,000.00 but an inventory at the probate of the will showed only $2,149.75. After debts were paid only, $719.20 remained. Jackson received nothing because of a law that prevents a person from willing real-estate to their lovers. But by some legal maneuvering the court finally awarded Jackson $71.92.

After the death of Kate Townsend, the authorities and newspapers, in quest of heirs to her considerable fortune, managed to put together a sketchy account of her brief career before she came to New Orleans. Public Administrator's Office learned her real name was Katherine Cunningham, that she had never married and that she was born in Liverpool, England, in 1837, the daughter of a dock laborer. She was, at fifteen, a barmaid in a tough dance-house on Paradise Street in Liverpool. According to her own story, she remained a virgin until she was almost seventeen. She finally yielded to Peter Kearnayan, a handsome young sailor whose life she probably saved by knocking out two ruffians with a pewter mug, who had attacked him in the dance-house. Several months after Kearnagham sailed away, twins were born to her. When he returned, she gave him a beating and complained to the police. He was arrested and remained in jail for six months. She abandoned the twins, assumed the name of Townsend and came to America. She arrived in New Orleans in 1857, and immediately went to work at Clara Fisher's brothel on Canal Street between Basin and Rampart (the former Loews State Theater building now occupies that space). Her next move was Maggie Thompson's place on Customhouse Street, the last in which she was just one of the girls.

When Kate Townsend came to New Orleans at the age of

eighteen, she was a very pretty girl with an exceptionally fine figure, and was regarded as the most popular young strumpet of her time. But in later years she became very fat, weighing around three hundred pounds when she died. And according to the States, "When they cut her open the fat was seen to be six inches thick". Around the 1970s she began drinking heavily and putting on flesh. Her bosoms became very large and never failed to draw attention in the red-light district. But during her early years "on the turf" as the saying went, she was hefty but beautiful. When she was twenty-five, she was able to leave Maggie Thompson's and open a place of her own on Villere and Customhouse Street. She made influential friends among politicians and city officials, and with their help built the three-story palace at #40 Basin Street - probably the most luxurious brothels that ever opened its doors in the U.S.A. Kate reserved a suite of large rooms on the Common Street side of the building for her own occupancy. It's needless to say the decor and furnishings left nothing to be desired. This is what the Picayune had to say, in part, about the sleeping quarters of the mistress of the bordello,

"In the left hand corner there were, the works of renowned artists and small articles betraying good taste, both in selection and arrangement. A finely carved, small marble table stood, while adjoining this was a splendid glass door armoire, on the shelves of which were stored a plethora of finest linen wear and bed clothing. Over the mantel was costly French mirror with gilt frame. A large sideboard stood in the corner next to the window in which was stored a large quantity of silverware. The hangings of the bed, over the mosquito bar were lace, and on exquisite basket of flowers hung suspended from the tester of the bed. Around the walls were suspended chaste and costly oil paintings.

The remainder of the house was furnished with the same type of magnificent. The building and it's contents were said to have cost over a hundred thousand dollars. High-class trade only was welcome. Rowdies who occasionally invaded #40 Basin Street was promptly ejected by Kate Thompson in person.. She was strong and very dangerous when aroused, and acted as her own bouncer. There were from fifteen to twenty girls on regular duty. Each had one day off a week, which she usually spent at the theater or drinking in the cafes with her "fancy man". Kate insisted that all her girls must wear evening gowns when on duty. No bawdy talk and behavior were allowed. Everyone was required to be a "lady to her fingertips". A spade was never called a spade, in Kate's place.

When a gentleman arrived he was met at the door by a uniformed Negro maid. If he was one of the steady clients, many of whom had charge accounts, he was ushered into the drawing-room where he was expected to buy wine, from ten to fifteen dollars a bottle, for everyone in the room. If he was a stranger, he was shown into a smaller room and questioned by Kate, while they drank a glass of wine together, at about two dollars a glass. If his credentials were in order he was then escorted into the drawing-room and formally presented to the ladies by his first name. If one of the ladies appealed to him, he would let Kate know, who in turn would inform the lucky Strumpet. If she was willing, and it would be hard to imagine one not being willing, she would discreetly leave the drawing-room and return to her boudoir. Shortly thereafter, the gentleman was conducted to her boudoir. The price for this adventure was fifteen dollars. Kate herself was sometime available for the entertainment of a particularly distinguished client, which is said to have been at a price of fifty dollars an hour. Kate's business prospered for about six years until her carpetbag politicians friends power began to wove. She was forced to curtail some of her strictest rules and make reduction in her rates, which means the brothel begin to accept men of less wealth and importance. This did not set well with Kate, to have to lower her standards. She became increasingly mean and bad tempered, which helped to drive away trade.

In 1870, Kate's place suffered a severe temporary set-back, when Gres Taney, a young gambler, who was noted for the number of weapons he carried on his person, a derringer, a revolver, a Bowie knife, a sling shot, and a gimlet knife, was murdered in the drawing-room by Jim White also a gambler. On the night of July 30th, Taney and White visited Kate Townsend's place and Taney ordered a bottle of wine at ten dollars. When he started to pay he found he had only two dollars and a half. "Never mind", said Kate "you can pay for it some other time". White then said, "I can whip any damn bastard that can't pay for the wine", Taney accused White of stealing his money, and White lunged at him. Taney drew his revolver, but before he could use it White stabbed him in the heart with a knife, it had a nine inch blade which he carried in a red sheath beneath his armpit. The revolver was found on the floor by the police, who gave it and the knife to Kate Townsend as a souvenir. She used to sleep with the knife under her pillow and carried it on her person, when she was herself finally murdered by Treville Egbert Sykes, the some of a merchant and auctioneer of Magazine Street. She had met Sykes, who was known as Bill, when she was a Strumpet in a brothel on Canal Street and he was a "fancy man", for almost twenty-five years.

Skyes wasn't much in evidence during Kate's youthful years but he becomes increasingly prominent in her affairs after she had lost her youth and beauty. He moved into the brothel in 1878 in a small room on the 2nd floor. In return for his board and lodging he was suppose to keep the accounts, bring customers to the house, and make himself useful. He lived there for five years, during which time Kate led him a dog's life. According to Sykes, she would beat him, lock him in hark closets, gave him no spending money, and once almost cut his nose off with her knife. She was always threatening to "open his belly". She claimed he was jealous and a thief. Just a few months after he moved in the brothel she had him arrested for forging her name to five checks totaling seven thousand dollars, but she didn't press charges and refused to prosecute.

Kate and Sykes troubles escalated about the middle of October 1883, when she became infatuated with a young "fancy man", named McLern, who came often to the house to borrow money and secure other favors from the Madame. Sykes protested and tried to kick McLern out. He was severely beaten by his mistress and her new lover. The day after this incident Kate was in the kitchen with Molly Johnson, a St. Louis girl, when she picked up a heavy butcher knife and said, "I've a good mind to take this knife and open Sykes' belly". Molly Johnson talked her out of that notion. Instead she called Sykes to the kitchen where she beat him with a bread board.

On Thursday night, November 1, 1883, Kate and Molly met McLern and another man on Canal Street and the four got drunk in Pizzini's Cafe', where Kate and McLern quarreled and McLern threatened her with a champagne bottle. He apologized when Kate drew her knife and said, "I've got to cut somebody, I'll go home and open Sykes' belly".

When they returned to Basin Street, Molly warned Sykes who locked and barred his door.

Kate remained in her suite for two days, sleeping off her hangover. On Saturday morning, November 3, Sykes arose and went to Kate's room. The housekeeper, Mary Philomine, a Negro woman, heard screams and found Sykes and Kate fighting in the bedroom. Sykes put the servant out and locked the door. According to the servant, she then heard shrieks and "terrible noises" coming from the room. After several minutes the door opened and Sykes appeared, bleeding from cuts on the left breast and below the left knee. "Well, Mary" he said, "She's gone"!

A few hours later the States reported:

"At half ten this morning a report was spread on St. Charles Street, among the sporting fraternity, that Kate Townsend, Madame of the brothel at 40 Basin Street, had been murdered by Treville Sykes, her lover".

At first everyone thought it was a joke, but when the police arrived they found Kate lying halfway across the elegant bed with her feet resting on the floor. She was covered with blood, her body having been pierced by four stab wounds, apparently inflicted with a broad knife. Next morning the "Picayune" published an account of the murder under these headlines:

"Carved to Death! Terrible Fate of Kate Townsend at the Hands of Treville Sykes With the Instrumentality of a Bowie Knife. Her Breasts and Shoulders Literally Covered with Stabs".

Sykes told the police that soon after he entered her room Kate drew the knife from under her pillow and attacked him. He wrenched the knife from her grasp. She grabbed a pair of pruning shears and continued the attack. He killed her then in self-defense.

Kate's body, decked out in a six-hundred dollar white silk dress, trimmed with fifteen dollars a yard lace, was laid out in the drawing room. At the funeral on November 5, all the furniture was covered with white silk instead of the usual linen or muslin. Champagne was served to the guests in accordance with Kate's request. She was buried in a four-hundred dollar metallic casket. One corner of the casket bore a silver cross inscribed with her name, the date of her death and her age. The body was followed to Metaric Cemetery by a procession of twenty carriages. There was not a man in any of them. The Public Administrator took charge of the brothel and soon afterwards, No. 40 Basin Street was leased to Molly Johnson who operated it until her death in 1889, when the contents were sold at public auction and the place was closed. Eventually the Elks owned the property.

Treville Sykes was tried for murder and acquitted. He then produced a will dated September 9, 1873 in which Kate willed him her entire estate. The will went to Probate and Sykes was appointed executor. He was removed in February 1884 for violating some court order. At the same time, the Attorney-General asked the court to deprive Sykes of all interest in the estate except one-tenth of the movables on the grounds that he and Kate had lived in open concerbinage. Sykes fought vigorously but lost. The estate was finally settled in 1888. It amounted to $81,936.45, but the Mascot, a tabloid of the times, said this was whittled down and hocus-pocused with until only $33,142.65 went to the state treasury. Lawyers got about $30,000 of this difference and the rest went for court costs and other expenses. Sykes share was $34.00.

Fanny Sweet was an important figure in the field of professional strumpeting. She was also adventurous, e.g. Voodoo Practitioner, a Confederate spy and a dangerous and bad-tempered woman who carried a knife and two (2) pistols. She slept with both under her pillow. According to the True Delta,:

"A modern Lucretia Borgia ..., a hardened murderess...one of the most remarkable female desperadoes ever known."

At the height of her notoriety, about 1862, it was believed that Fanny had shot one man, poisoned three or four others, and that she regularly tortured her slaves. She was physically unattractive. She was about five feet ten inches tall, with a lumpy figure, large feet and hands, big nose, bushy eyebrows and very noticeable mustache. In spit of all these seemingly disadvantages, men seemed unable to resist her "skill in amour" as they would say. She never lacked a lover, and she left a trail of broken hearts from New Orleans to California and from California to New York.

The True Delta published a kind of expose' of Fanny Sweet on December 8 1861. It said her real name was Mary Robinson and that she had been born in a small town in New York in 1827. At the age of fifteen she went to New York City and began calling herself Fanny Smith and became known as one of the toughest little strumpets the Madames of New York had ever met. She was kicked out of at least six brothels for fighting. She came to New Orleans in 1844 and found work at a brothel on Dauphine Street between Canal and Customhouse. She was fired after a few weeks when she hurled one of the girls down the stairs and broke numerous bones in her body. Fanny then went to work at a large brothel on Royal Street. While there she caught the eye of a young banker who became infatuated with her. She quit the brothel job and became the banker's personal mistress. Shortly thereafter the banker stole a large sum of money from his bank and fled to Havana. Fanny Sweet answered The True Delta's expose' with what she called the true story - The autobiography of Mrs. Fanny Sweet: A Card to the Public which the newspaper published in two installments on December 10, 1861. She said she was born in England, the only child of parents who reared her in comfort and luxury. She did not divulge her real name or the exact place of her birth. Her father and mother died when she was eight (8) years old and she was brought to American by a family which settled on a farm in the Guyandot region of West Virginia. After about 6 years, (at age 15) her foster parents placed her in the hands of a gentleman relative who promised to take her to a boarding school in

Cincinnati. Instead he seduced her and for two years she waited for him to marry her as he had promised. Finally they were to come to New Orleans. They booked passage on a steamboat. At Memphis he got off to attend to some business as he explained. When the boat left Memphis, he had not returned. This was in 1846. When she arrived in New Orleans she went to live with a man and his wife whom she had met on the boat and who operated a book store in Exchange Alley. When they learned the truth of her situation they cast her out. A lawyer who offered to help soon tired of her. She had no recourse but the bordellos. From this point the stories of Fanny Sweet and The True Delta are substantially in agreement. She strongly denied receiving any money from the banker who ran away to Havana. She was, at that time, supported very liberally by a wealthy gentleman, Mr. P., whom she met by appointment at the house of an old woman named Moss...

Mr. P. Vanished from the scene in 1849, when Fanny went to New York (her first visit there) then on to California in the company of two respectable lady friends. She ran a haberdashery, at big profit in San Francisco until the fire of May 4, 1850. She then went to Sacramento and became the mistress of the owner of a large building part of which she operated as a boarding-house. "These were rough, lawless times in California" said The True Delta, "but she was rougher and more lawless than any... she became feared even among the miners with whom she mixed as if a man, always armed to the teeth. She had many fights. She shot a stage driver dead, and in another encounter she had three of her ribs broken." Fanny Sweet's trouble with stage drivers and miners culminated late in 1852 when a mob invaded her home and destroyed the furniture. She protested and a man name Putman slapped her, where upon she drew her pistol and shot him dead. She was tried by a Justice of the Peace and acquitted, and a gang of rowdies demolished the Justice's house. They threatened to hang Fanny Sweet, but she escaped while the noose was being prepared and hid in a prison brig moored in the Sacramento River.

A grand jury indited her, but she left early in 1853 and returned to New Orleans and published a card announcing that she had abandoned her wicked ways and wished to be received as a respectable lady. The response was negative and she was offended. After a few weeks she went to Panama. There she married Abraham M. Hinkley, wealthy owner of Hinkley's California Express. She appeared again in New Orleans in 1854 with lots of cash and bought a large brick house on St. Louis Street, with six Negroes and a gaudy carriage in which she drove about clad in silk and satin, bedecked in jewels. She was charged in 1855 with mistreating her slaves but was vindicated. She soon went to New York and divorced Hinkley in 1856. He went to Nicaragua soon after her filing and was killed by a Nicaraguan at Grenada.

In 1860 Fanny again appeared in New Orleans and situated herself in a small house on Canal Street. It was then she began to embrace Voodooism. She attended many of the secret meetings of the cult, did business with the famous Voodoo Queen Marie Laveau and the voodoo doctors. She believed she had acquired the power through voodooism, to produce effects. Her first victim, a Mr. M. whom The True Delta described as "a gentleman of years and means, of high standing in both social and business circles". He lavished his wealth upon her. He gave her a house located on Gasquet and Basin Streets, furnishing it with perfect taste, stocking it with the finest wine and imported liquors, colored servants, a carriage that was built to order in New Jersey, fast horses and everything she would want at her disposal. In this house where she and Mr. M. Were known as Mr. and Mrs. Sweet, she lived for two years. He visited the house two or three times a week. During this time period she operated, unknown to Mr. M., a select bordello providing young girls for the amusement of elderly men and then blackmailing the latter, one of whom paid her ten thousand dollars in less than a year.

When Mr. M. Learned what was going on, he tried to break with Fanny; but she laughed and convinced him she could ruin him is she wished by exerting her Voodoo powers. He offered her a large sum of money to leave New Orleans. She took the money, but didn't leave. Instead, she asked for more money, but when he refused, she prophesied that he would fall ill. In a day or so he did become ill with a sickness that mystified doctors who called his illness "congestive chills". He recovered only after he had summoned Fanny and paid through the nose for a "secret remedy."

He thereafter took care of all her expenses without protest until she found his successor, a very rich William G. Stephens, a widower with two children. He was known as a tightwad and drove a shabby buggy drawn by a little mule. He also was a very religious man, careful of his good name. According to The True Delta, he would not enter a coffee house much less enter a bordello. This high-minded gentleman fell hard for Fanny Sweet and she became his mistress within a week. To protect his reputation she closed her Gasquet Street house and began wearing men's clothing thereafter until the end of the adventure, loved openly in the Stephen's mansion as his nephew Freddy and was introduced as such to his business friends. She accompanied him on trips. She also supervised the education of Stephens' children and controlled the household expenditures which increased enormously. In August 1861 she made a business trip to New York for her lover, and while there she obtained valuable information which she sold to the Confederate authorities.

When she returned from New York, she persuaded Stephens to turn all his assets into cash and pool their resources, travel to Mexico and buy quinine and munitions of war, and then bring these supplies back into Texas and Louisiana and sell them to the Confederate Army. Stephens seeing the possibility of a large profit, quickly agreed. On November 1, 1861, they left New Orleans accompanied by a man named Lincoln, one of Stephens employees. They had with them the pooled purse of about sixty-five thousand dollars. Most of which Stephens had contributed. Somewhere between Houston and Corpus Christi, Texas, Stephens suddenly fell ill with "congestive chills" and died. Stephens was quickly buried in a tin box. Fanny Sweet and Lincoln headed back to Louisiana with the sixty-five thousand dollars. However, reports had reached New Orleans that Stephens had been poisoned by Fanny Sweet and that she was not headed for Louisiana but in flight through Mexico with Lincoln. The True Delta, writing about the incident, remarked that Lincoln's life "would not be insured at this time for ninety-nine cents on the dollar by any insurance company in the city and the chances of him succumbing to 'congestive chills' before they got half-way to Vera Cruz was fifty to one."

The police searched the house on Gasquet Street and found a voodoo casket in which were several packets of white powder, believed to have been love potions if not poison and a lock of bloodstained hair, one of the most potent of Voodoo charms. Fanny Sweet said the powder was medicine and that the lock of hair had been taken from Hinkley's scalp "while the warm blood was yet trickling over it," and sent to her by one of his Nicaraguan friends. Anyway, the investigator broke down, insufficient evidence. The Attorney General announced officially that Fanny was innocent of any connection with Stephen's death. While the <u>Picayune</u> said there was "nothing against Fanny but her past reputation".

Fanny Sweet vanished from New Orleans when the Yankees captured the city and is believed to have spent the next few years in New York, Washington and other northern cities as a Confederate spy. She returned at the close of the war, opened her house on Gasquet Street and lived there for almost twenty years. She got into no serious trouble. She attended strictly to her business of running a high class bordello. She left New Orleans in 1889, when she was about sixty years old and is believed to have died a few years later in Florida.

During the time of the rise and fall of Kate Townsend, Hattie Hamilton and Fanny Sweet, the lowest of cheap parlor houses and cribs could be found on Dauphine, Burgundy, St. Louis, Conti, Customhouse and Bienville Streets in the French Quarter; and in the American section on Franklin Street, which ran from Basin Street to Claiborne Avenue a block above Canal Street. The worst dive on Gasquet Street was a twenty-five cent crib-house called Pig-Trough Carries, while on Franklin Street you could find such notorious dives as McCarthy's Ranch, the Picayune House and a combination dance-hall and gambling-den at #22 which was a hangout for Negro burglars and footpads. In the rear of #22 Franklin, Kendrick Hollard, A Negro Monte dealer ran a lunch room where his mistress Hannah Glover worked the kitchen when she was not busy in the brothel division of the establishment. Hannah enjoyed playing a card game called seven-up, but she wasn't good at the game. Kendrick would stand behind her and offer advice. He became annoyed at her continued lack of skill and while watching her on the evening of August 17, 1883, he suddenly leaned forward and tapped her on the shoulder and said, "I'll kill you if you don't do better than that". On the next deal Hannah made a stupid play and Holland drew a pistol and shot her in the back of the head. "I told her I'd do it", he said, "but she wouldn't believe me".

Around the Dauphine and Burgundy vice areas, white and black women lived together indiscriminately and were patronized by men of all races and colors, a situation which persisted for many years before and after the Civil War. This is what a publication called the <u>Lantern</u> had to say in May 22, 1888:

"In our daily walks through life, we notice the surprising amount of co-habitation of white men and Negro women".

On November 30, 1889 the <u>Mascot</u> presented the other side of the picture by declaring:

"This thing of white girls becoming enamored of Negroes is becoming rather too common".

The whole area swarmed with street walkers and their "fancy men" and since street walkers rarely had permanent quarters, they did not hesitate in throwing a piece of old carpet on the sidewalk and entertaining their customers in full view of passers-by. The strumpets with quarters looked down from their windows screaming abuse at the street walkers and keeping pails of hot water handy to discourage the street walkers from using the door steps. Inside the bordello, prices were from fifteen to fifty cents; on the sidewalks the standard rate was ten cents. Many of these women were addicted to flagellation and their needs were served by a professional flagellant called Joe the Whipper, who was a familiar figure around Dauphine and Burgundy Streets for years.

Number 111 Dauphine Street was described by the <u>Picayune</u>, in 1885, as the worst Negro dive in the city and was the hang-out of a strumpet called Red Light Liz, the sweetheart of Joe the

Whipper, and a noted brawler. In the earlier days, however, the house had been occupied by white prostitutes. It gained considerable renown because of the tragic end of one of its girls, Nellie Gaspar.

Nellie Gaspar, the daughter of a London innkeeper, came to New Orleans in 1866. She was seduced by a smooth talker who then put her in the Dauphine Street brothel. She soon moved to a house on Treme Street. After a few weeks she moved to a brothel on Custom House Street operated by Madame Schneider, who was noted for her terrible temper. Meanwhile, Nellie's seducer had left her and she had taken a new lover. After a few days at Madame Schneider's the man who had seduced her broke into her room, stole all of her money and beat her unmercifully with the butt of a pistol. She was still alive when found by Madame Schneider who put her in a small room and traded her water for dresses until her wardrobe was gone. She was then sent to Charity Hospital but was discharged after three days and returned to the brothel at No. 111 Dauphine Street where she died within a week.

On Burgundy Street, between Bienville and Conti, was known as Smoky Rowe Notorious during the early 1870's because of almost continuous fighting of four tough strumpets known as Kidney-Foot Jenny, Fighting Mary, One-eyed Sal and Gallus Lu. For at least twenty years dives on Smoky Row operated filled with prostitutes of all ages from ten years old to seventy. When not fighting or otherwise occupied, they sat in door-ways, behind blinds or in front of small alley-ways leading to the rear of the house. Whenever a man passed they tried to drag him inside, robbed him, beat him and threw him back into the street.

As recently as the early 1930s this writer can recall an incident happening not much unlike what's noted on Smoky Row:

My Uncle Charley Johnson (most people called him "Creep" affectionately) was a large George Forman-like man with a booming baritone voice and a healthy belly-laugh. He worked for the O.K. Storage Company in New Orleans as a piano mover mostly. After a hard day's work, a bath, six pork chops, fixed dry and brown with rice and a hoe cake, he liked to put on his silk shirt, box straw and two-tone shoes and go for a stroll in the cool of the evening with me, a thirteen year old and my friend Woodrow who was about sixteen years old. We usually walked out Gravier Street headed toward Rampart Street. "Creep" knew just about everyone on the street, strumpets included. Nothing seemed to make him happier than when he was exchanging greetings and laughs with people on both sides of the street. One day, he looked back chuckling on me and my friend, Woodrow. I was there but Woodrow wasn't. There were a few bordellos situated on Gravier Street along our route; and one of the "girls" had snatched Woodrow. People on the opposite side of the street saw what happened and pointed out the house to "Creep". "Creep" went in at once and retrieved Woodrow "before any damage was done" as he likes to tell it. He then proceeded to give the strumpet a very loud tongue-lashing ending with, "Don't you ever, ever, ever do that again, you must have known this boy was with me". To my knowledge, it never happened again.

Another flourishing business that went on at the same time the bordellos were in full bloom was called procuring. These procuresses supplied girls for the bordellos in Galveston, Atlanta, Memphis and other Southern cities. A school teacher named Louisa Murphy is reported to have sold several young girls during the late 1860s for around eight hundred dollars each.

Mary Thompson was operating on Royal Street in the middle 1840s with a cigar store as a blind. She specialized in virgins whom she sold for from two hundred to four hundred dollars each. In March 1845, Mary was en route to a Burgundy Street house to deliver a girl she had sold to an elderly man for three hundred and fifty dollars, when the girl broke away. Mary had her arrested on a charge of stealing. The case was dismissed and the girl brought suit against Mary for attempting to injure her character. She was awarded fifty dollars damages and the police warned Mary that if she tried to sell another girl she might be punished. Competition was so keen that about 1880 a virgin could be bought for about fifty dollars. Leaders in the field at this time were Nellie Haley of Custom House Street, Miss Carol of Baronne Street, Mother Mansfield of Bienville Street and

Spanish Agnes of Burgundy Street. While Miss Carol carried on a general procuring business in girls and women, she also operated a profitable side line - she found boys for the amusements of male degenerates. Miss Carol is said to have been the financial backer of an assignation house on Lafayette Street near Buronne for their convenience. Carol installed a Mister who called himself Miss Big Nellie. Both black and whit men were invited to frequent balls given at the house. Miss Big Nellie had a fifteen-year-old boy for sale. He offered him at a bargain to a <u>Mascot</u> reporter who was investigating the activities of the operations. When the reporter refused to buy, Big Nellie cried,"

"You're a fool! The boy's a virgin! You'll never get another chance like this in New Orleans.

Chapter IV

The Plague

He came to New Orleans aboard a steamboat from Louisville in 1821. His name was Theodore Clapp, a Presbyterian preacher. He admits in his memoir that he was prejudiced against New Orleans before he saw it, for he had heard stories that the city was not unlike Sodom. However, in time he changed his mind and he eventually came to love New Orleans as he had never loved a city before. All this he tells in detail in his memoir. Dr. Clapp is important to historians because he gives a first-hand account of the great devastating plague of 1832. Since the volume is so rare now, I shall quote this remarkable broad-minded and clear-eyed man at length:

"The previous summer (he writes), in the month of August, a frightful tornado had swept over and inundated New Orleans. The Creoles said that this was the forerunner of some frightful pestilence. I proposed to leave Mrs. Clapp and the children with her aunt in Kentucky, till the overflowing scourge should pass through the land. But she declined....

We arrived at New Orleans, on our return home, about the first of September. The weather was most sultry and oppressive. TO most of my friends out conduct appeared so unwise, that they hardy gave us a cordial welcome back....That very week, several cases of yellow fever occurred in the Charity Hospital and boarding houses along the levee. It soon grew into an epidemic and carried off hundreds during this and the succeeding month.

On the morning of the 25th of October, 1832, as I was walking home from market, before sunrise, I saw two men lying on the levee in a dying condition. They had been landed from a steamboat which arrived the night before. Some of the watchmen had gone after a handbarrow or cart, on which they might be removed to the hospital. At first there was quite a crowd assembled on the spot. But an eminent physician rode up in his gig, and gazing a moment, exclaimed in a loud voice, "Those men have the Asiatic cholera." The crowd dispersed in a moment, and ran as if for their lives in every direction. I was left almost alone with the sufferers. They could speak, and were in full possession of their reason. They had what I afterwards found were the usual symptoms of cholera - cramps, convulsions, $c. The hands and feet were cold and blue; an icy perspiration flowed in streams; and they complained of a great pressure upon their chests. One of them said it seemed as if a bar of iron was lying across him. Their thirst was intense, which caused an insufferable agony in the mouth and throat. They entreated me to procure some water. I attempted to go on board the steamboat which had put them on shore. But the staging had been drawn in to prevent all intercourse with people on the levee. Thence I returned, intending to go to the nearest dwelling to get some relief for the unhappy men, whom all but God had apparently deserted.

At that instant the watchmen arrived with a dray. Happily (because, perhaps, they spoke only the French language), they had no suspicion that these strangers were suffering from the cholera. If I had pronounced that terrific word in their hearing, they too might have fled, and left the sick men to perish on the cold ground. I saw them placed on the vehicle, and subsequently leaned that they were corpses before eleven o'clock A.M. the same day.

I walked home, attempting to be calm and resigned, determined to do my duty, and leave the consequences with God. I said nothing to my family about the sick men whom I had met, though they thought it strange that I had taken so much more time than usual in going to and from the market, and observed that I looked uncommonly thoughtful and serious. I felt that the hour of peril had come....

The weather, this morning, was very peculiar. The heavens were covered with thick, heavy, damp, lowering clouds, that seemed like one black ceiling, spread over the whole horizon. To the eye, it almost touched the tops of the houses. Every one felt a strange difficulty of respiration. I never looked upon such a gloomy, appalling sky before or since. Not a breath of wind stirred. It was so dark, that in some of the banks, offices, and private houses, candles or lamps were lighted that day.

Immediately after breakfast I walked down to the post office. At every corner, and around the principal hotels, were groups of anxious faces. As soon as they saw me, the question was put by several persons at a time, "Is it a fact that the cholera is in the city?" I replied by describing what I had seen but two hours before. Observing that many of them appeared panic-struck, I remarked, "Gentlemen, do not be alarmed. These may prove merely what the doctors call sporadic cases. We do not yet know that it will prevail to an alarming extent. Let us trust in God, and wait patiently the developments of another morning.

That day as many persons left the city as could find the means of transmigration. On my way home from the post office, I walked along the levee, where the two cholera patients had been disembarked but three or four hours before. Several families in the neighborhood were making preparations to move, but in vain. They could not obtain the requisite vehicles. The same afternoon the pestilence entered their houses, and before dark spread through several squares opposite to the point where the steamer landed the first cases.

On the evening of the 27th of October, it had made its way through every part of the city. During the ten succeeding days, reckoning from October 27 to the 6th of November, all the physicians judged that, at the lowest computation there were five thousand deaths - an average of five hundred every day. Many died of whom no account was rendered. A great number of bodies, with bricks and stones tied to the feet, were thrown into the river. Many were privately interred in gardens and enclosures, on the grounds where they expired, whose names were not recorded in the bills of mortality. Often I was kept in the burying ground for hours in succession, by the incessant, unintermitting arrival of corpses, over whom I was requested to perform a short service. One day, I did not leave the cemetery till nine o'clock at night; the last interments were made by candle light. Reaching my house faint, exhausted, horror-stricken, I found my family all sobbing and weeping, for they had concluded, from my long absence, that I was certainly dead.

I never went abroad without kissing and blessing them all, with the conviction that we should never meet again on earth. After bathing and taking some refreshment, I started out to visit the sick. My door was thronged with servants, waiting to conduct me to the rooms of dying sufferers. In this kind o labor I spend most of the night. At three o'clock A.M., I returned home, threw myself down on a sofa, with directions not to be called till half past five. I was engaged to attend a funeral at six o'clock A.M., 28th October....

The morning after, at six o'clock, I stepped into a carriage to accompany a funeral procession to the cemetery. On my arrival, I found at the graveyard a large pile of corpses without coffins, in horizontal layers, one above the other, like corded wood. I was told that there were more than one hundred bodies deposited there. They had been brought by unknown persons, at different hours since nine o'clock the evening previous. Large trenches were dug, into which these uncoffined corpses were thrown indiscriminately. The same day, a private hospital was found deserted; the physicians, nurses, and attendants were all dead, or had run away. Not a living person was in it. The wards were filled with putrid bodies, which, by order of the mayor, were piled in an adjacent yard, and burned, and their ashes scattered to the winds. Could a wiser disposition have been made of them?

Many persons, even of fortune and popularity, died in their beds without aid, unnoticed and unknown, and lay there for days unburied. In almost every house might be seen the sick, the dying, and the dead, in the same room. All the stores, banks, and places of business were closed. There were no means, no instruments for carrying on the ordinary affairs of business; for all the drays, carts, carriages, hand and common wheel-barrows, as well as hearses, were employed in the transportation of corpses, instead of cotton, sugar, and passengers. Words cannot describe my sensations when I firs beheld the awful sight of carts driven to the graveyard, and there upturned, and their contents discharged as so many loads of lumber or offal, without a single mark of mourning or respect, because the exigency rendered it impossible.

The Sabbath came, and I ordered the sexton to ring the bell

for church at eleven o'clock A.M., as usual. I did not expect to meet a half a dozen persons; but there was actually a congregation of two or three hundred, and all gentlemen. The ladies were engaged in taking care of the sick. There was no singing. I made a very short prayer, and preached a discourse not more than fifteen minutes in length. It made such an impression that several of the hearers met me at the door, and requested me to write it down for their perusal and meditation. I complied with the request. My text was the passage found in Isaiah, XXVI, 3: "Thou wilt keep him in perfect peace whose mind is stayed on thee, because he trusteth in thee."

For several days after this Sabbath, the plague raged with unabated violence. But the events, toils, trials, and gloom of one day, in this terrific visitation, were a *fac-simile* of those that characterized the whole scene. A fatal yellow fever had been spreading destruction in the city six weeks before the cholera commenced. Thousands had left it to escape this scourge. So that, at the time of the first cholera, it was estimated that the population of the city did not exceed thirty-five thousand inhabitants. During the entire epidemic, at least six thousand persons perished; showing the frightful loss of one sixth of the people in about twelve days. This is the most appalling instance of mortality known to have happened in any part of the world, ancient or modern. Yet, in all the accounts of the ravages of this enemy, in 1832, published in the northern cities and Europe, its desolations in New Orleans are not even noticed - a fact which requires no comment. The same ratio of mortality in Boston, the next twelve days, would call for more than twenty-three thousand victims. Who can realize this truth? The same epidemic broke out again the following summer, in June 1833. In September of the same year, the yellow fever came back again. So, within the space of twelve months, we had two Asiatic choleras, and two epidemic yellow fevers, which carried off ten thousand persons that were known, and many more that were not reported.

Multitudes began the day in apparently good health, and were corpses before sunset. One morning, as I was going out, I spoke to a gentleman who resided in the very next house to mine. He was standing at his door, and remarked that he felt very well; "but I wonder," he added, "that you are alive." On my return, only two hours afterwards, he was a corpse. A baker died in his cart directly before my door. Near me there was a brick house going up; two of the workmen died on a carpenter's bench, but a short time after they had commenced their labors of the day. Often did it happen that a person engaged a coffin for some friend, who himself died before it could be finished. On a certain evening, about dark, a gentleman called on me to say a short service over the body of a particular friend just deceased: the next morning I performed the same service for him. I went one Wednesday night, to solemnize the contract of matrimony between a couple of very genteel appearance. The bride was young and possessed of the most extraordinary beauty. A few hours only had elapsed before I was summoned to perform the last offices over her coffin. She had on her bridal dress, and was very little changed in the appearance of her face.

Three married gentlemen, belonging to my congregation, lived together and kept bachelor's hall, as it is termed with us. I was called to visit one of them at ten o'clock P.M.. He lived but a few moments after I entered the room. Whilst I was conversing with the survivors, a second brother was taken with cramps. There was nobody in the house but the servants. They were especially dear to me because of their intrinsic character, and because they were regular attendants at church We instantly applied the usual remedies, but without success. At one o'clock in the morning he breathed his last. The only surviving brother immediately fell beside the couch of the lifeless ones, and at daylight he died. We laid the three corpses side by side.

One family, of nine persons, supped together in perfect health; at the expiration of the next twenty-four hours, eight out of the nine were dead. A boarding house, that contained thirteen inmates, was absolutely emptied; not one was left to mourn.

Persons were found dead all along the streets, particularly early in the mornings. For myself, I expected that the city would be depopulated. I have no doubt, that if the truth could be ascertain, it would appear that those persons who died so suddenly were affected with what are called the premonitory symptoms hours, perhaps a day, or a night, before they considered themselves unwell. In this early stage, the disease is easily arrested; but when the cramps and collapse set in, death is, in most cases, inevitable. Indeed, that is death. *Then*, nothing was known of the cholera, and its antecedent stages were unnoticed and uncared for. Hence, in a great measure, the suddenness as well s the extent of the mortality.

Nature seemed to sympathize in the dreadful spectacle of human woe. A thick, dark atmosphere, as I said before, hung over us like a mighty funeral shroud. All was still. Neither sun, nor moon, nor stars shed their blessed light. Not a breath of air moved. A hunter, who lived on the bayou St. John, assured me that during the cholera he killed no game. Not a bird was seen winging the sky. Artificial causes of terror were superadded to the gloom which covered the heavens. The burning of tar and pitch at every corner; the firing of cannon, by order of the city authorities, along all the streets; and the frequent conflagrations which actually occurred at that dreadful period - all these conspired to add a sublimity and horror to the tremendous scene. Our wise men hoped, by the combustion of tar and gunpowder, to purify the atmosphere. We have no doubt that hundreds perished from mere fright produced by artificial noise, the constant sight of funerals, darkness, and various other causes.

It was an awful spectacle to see night ushered in by the firing of artillery in different parts of the city, making as much noise as arises from the engagement of two powerful armies. The sight was one of the most tremendous which was every presented to the eye, or even exhibited to the imagination, in description. Often, walking my nightly rounds, the flames from the burning tar so illuminated the city streets and river, that I could see everything almost as distinctly as in the daytime. And through many a window into which was flung the sickly flickering of these conflagrations, could be seen persons struggling in death, and rigid, blackened corpses, awaiting the arrival of some cart or hearse, s soon as dawn appeared, to transport them to their final resting place.

During these ineffable, inconceivable horrors, I was enabled to maintain my post for fourteen days, without a moment's serious illness. I often sank down upon the floor, sofa, or pavement, faint or exhausted from over-exertion, sleeplessness, and want of food; but a short nap would partially restore me, and send me out afresh to renew my perilous labors. For a whole fortnight, I did not attempt to undress except to bathe and put on clean apparel. I was like a soldier, who is not allowed, by the constant presence of an enemy, to throw off his armor, and lay down his weapons for a single moment. Morning, noon, and midnight, I was engaged in the sick room, and in performing services over the dead. The thought that I myself should be exempted from the scourge - how could it be cherished for a moment? I expected that every day would be my last. Yet, as I said before, I did not have the slightest symptom of the cholera....

My escape was wonderful, considered in another respect. For fifteen days in succession, the atmosphere was loaded with the most deadly malaria, and every species of noxious impurity. I had to encounter not only the general insalubrity which always infects the air when cholera prevails, but to this were superadded the constant inhalations of the sick-bed effluvium which emanates from corpses in every stage of decomposition, in which life had been extinct for days, perhaps, and the offensive smells of the cemetery. Most of the bodies laid in the ground had a covering of earth but a few inches in depth, and through the porous dust there was an unimpeded emission of all the gases evolved from animal matter, when undergoing the process of putrefaction. The sick poor were often crowed together in low, narrow, damp, basement, unventilated rooms.

Many times, on entering these apartments, and putting my head under the mosquito bar, I became deadly sick in a moment, and was taken with vomiting, which, however, passed off without producing serious effects in a single instance. Let the reader imagine a close room, in which are lying half a dozen bodies in the process of decay, and he may form a faint conception of the physical horrors in which I lived, moved, and had my being continually for two entire weeks. My preservation has always seemed to me like a miracle. It is true, some constitutions are not susceptible of the cholera. Some can never take the yellow fever or small pox. It is not improbable that my safety ought to be ascribed to some peculiar idiosyncrasy, which enabled me to breathe the air of this plague with impunity.

In 1822, I knew an unacclimated gentleman who slept on the same bed with an intimate friend, whilst he was sick of the yellow fever: on the morning of his death, he himself, his clothes, and the sheets, were absolutely inundated by a copious discharge of the *vomito.* After the funeral, he continued to occupy the same room, and had the best health all that summer and autumn. During the next thirty years, he never left the city for a day, and was never sick. I have known numerous instances of the kind....

The cholera had been raging with unabated fury for fourteen days. It seemed as if the city was destined to be emptied of its inhabitants. During this time, as before stated, a thick dark, sultry atmosphere filled our city. Every one complained of a difficulty in breathing, which he never before experienced. The heavens were as stagnant as the mantled pool of death. There were no breezes. At the close of the fourteenth day, about eight o'clock in the evening, a smart storm, something like a tornado, came from the north-west, accompanied with heavy peals of thunder and terrific lightnings. The deadly air was displaced immediately, bu that which was new, fresh, salubrious, and life-giving. The next morning shone forth all bright and beautiful. The plague was stayed. In the opinion of all the medical gentlemen who were on the spot, that change of weather terminated the epidemic. At any rate, it took its departure from us that very hour. No new cases occurred after that storm. It is certainly, then, in the power of God, not only by wind and electricity, but also by other means innumerable beyond our powers of discernment, to deliver a city from pestilence, in answer to the prayers of his children. Some one has said that, "a little philosophy may make one an unbeliever, but that a great deal will make him a Christian."...

In the cholera of June, 1833, the disease first invaded our own family circle. Two daughters, the eldest four, and the youngest two years of age, died about the same time. I was so fortunate as to procure a carriage, in which their bodies were conveyed to a family vault, in the Girod cemetery, which had been constructed and presented to me, some years before, by the trustees of Christ Church, Canal Street - a church characterized for large, generous, and noble sympathies. I rode in the carriage alone with the two coffins. There was not a soul present by myself, to aid in performing the last sad offices. Most desolate and heavy was my heart"....

Dr. Clapp remained in New Orleans through several plagues and epidemics. In the latter portion of his memoir, he continues his description: "Let me attempt to suggest a general but ver inadequate idea of my labors and sufferings in each of the campaigns above referred to. The term of a sickly season in New Orleans has never been less than six weeks. In a majority of cases it has extended from eight weeks to ten. In 1824, it began early in June, and did not entirely disappear till the November following. On an average, it is within bounds to say that the duration of each epidemic spoken of in these pages was at least eight weeks. Multiply eight by twenty, and the product is one hundred and sixty. Hence it follows that since my settlement in Louisiana I have spend over three entire years in battling, with all my might, against those invisible enemies, the cholera and yellow fever,. In these three years I scarcely enjoyed a night of undisturbed repose. When I did sleep, it was upon my post, in the midst of the dead and wounded, with my armor on, and ready at the first summons to meet the deadly assault....

Perhaps there is no acute disease actually less painful than yellow fever, although there is none more shocking and repulsive to the beholder. Often I have met and shook hands with some blooming, handsome young man to-day, and in a few hours afterwards, I have been called to see him with profuse hemorrhages from the mouth, nose, ears, eyes, and even the toes; the eyes prominent, glistening, yellow, and staring; the face discolored with orange color and dusky red.

The physiognomy of the yellow fever corpse is usually sad, sullen, and perturbed; the countenance dark, mottled, livid, swollen, and stained with blood and black vomit; the veins of the face and whole body become distended, and look as if they were going to burst; and though the heart has ceased to beat, the circulation of the blood sometimes continues for hours, quite as active as in life. Think reader, what it must be to have one's mind wholly occupied with such sights and scenes for weeks together, nay, more - for months, for years, for a whole lifetime even. Scarcely a night passes now, in which my dreams are not haunted more or less by the distorted faces, the shrieks, the convulsions, the groans, the struggles, and the horrors which I witnessed thirty-five years ago. They come up before my mind's eye like positive, absolute realities. I awake, rejoicing indeed to find that it is a dream; but there is no more sleep for me that night. No arithmetic could compute the diminution of my happiness, for the last forty years, from this single source. Setting aside another and better world to come, I would not make such a sacrifice as one epidemic demands, for all the fame, pleasures, and gold of earth. What, then will you think of twenty?

A clergyman said to me not long since, "You have indeed had a terrible time in New Orleans. You will be rewarded for it some time or other, but not *here*, not *here*. A suitable remuneration awaits you in the kingdom of God, beyond the grave."

I shocked my friend exceedingly by saying, "I neither expect any such remuneration nor desire it. I have had my reward already. Virtue is its own reward. I am no more entitle to a seat in heaven for all I have done (supposing my motives to have been holy) than the veriest wretch that ever expiated his crimes on the gallows." I repeat it, every person who does his duty receives a perfect recompense this side of the grave. He can receive nothing afterwards, except upon the platform of mercy. For the good deeds done in the body, there is no heaven but upon earth. When will Christian ministers learn this fundamental truth of the gospel?....

The two most fatal yellow fevers which I have witnessed were those of 1837 and 1853. In the former year there were ten thousand cases of fever reported, and five thousand deaths. The epidemic broke out about the middle of August, and lasted eight weeks. This is the greatest mortality which was ever known in the United States, if we expect that which occurred in the cholera of New Orleans, October, 1832. The year 1837 is memorable for the introduction of what is called the quinine practice. It is now, I am told by the physicians, generally abandoned. By some persons abroad, our doctors have been much blamed for thinking to overcome the yellow fever by the above-named medicine. For myself, I do not wonder that they made such an attempt. It had been recommended by the most celebrated practitioners in the West Indies, and in other tropical regions. New Orleans has always been blessed with the most learned, skilful, and competent physicians; but they are neither omniscient nor omnipotent. The cause of yellow fever is to this day a profound mystery...."

In writing of the epidemic of 1853, Dr. Clapp says: "On the day of my arrival, it rained incessantly from morning till night. In the space of twelve hours, the interments were over three hundred. The same day, I visited two unacclaimed families belonging to my own church, who were all down with the plague. In these families were nine persons; but two of them survived. I knew a large boarding house for draymen, mechanics, and humble operatives, from which forty-five corpses were borne away in thirteen days. A poor lady of my acquaintance kept boarders for a livelihood. Her family consisted of eight unacclimated persons. Every one of them died in the space of three weeks.

Six unacclimated gentlemen, intelligent, refined, and strictly temperate, used to meet once a week, to enjoy music, cheering conversation, and innocent amusements. They had been told that it was a great safeguard, in a sickly summer, to keep up good spirits, and banish from their minds dark and melancholy thoughts. They passed a certain evening together in health and happiness. In precisely one week from that entertainment, five of them were gathered to the tomb. One of the most appalling features of the yellow fever is the rapidity with which it accomplishes its mission.

There is some difficulty in arriving at the true statistics touching the epidemic of 1853. It was supposed by the best informed physicians that there were fifty or sixty thousand unacclimated persons in New Orleans when the epidemic began, about the 1st of July. From that time to the 1st of November, he whole number of deaths reported were ten thousand and three hundred. Of these eight thousand died of the yellow fever. The physicians estimated that thirty-two thousand of those attacked this year were cured. Of course, if this calculation be true, the whole number of cases in 1853 was forty thousand.

The horrors and desolations of this epidemic cannot be painted; neither can they be realized, except by those who have lived in New Orleans, and have witnessed and participated in similar scenes. Words can convey no adequate idea of them. In some cases, all the clerks and agents belonging to mercantile establishments were swept away, and the stores closed by the civil authorities. Several entire families were carried off - parents, children, servant, all. Others lost a quarter, or a third, or three fourths of their members, and their business, hopes, and happiness were blasted for life. The ravages of the destroyer were marked by more woeful and affecting varieties of calamity than were ever delineated on the pages of romance. Fifteen clergymen died that season - two Protestant ministers and thirteen Roman Catholic priests.

They were strangers to the climate, but could not be frightened from their posts of duty. The work *fear* was not in their vocabulary. Four Sisters of Charity were laid in their graves, and several others were brought to the point of death. It is painful to dwell on these melancholy details, but it may suggest profitable trains of thought. Set before your imaginations a picture of forty thousand persons engaged in a sanguinary battle, in which ten thousand men are killed outright. One thousand persons will fill a large church. Suppose ten congregations, of this number each, were to be assembled for worship in Boston, on the 1st day of July, 1858, and that on the first day of the following November, in the short space of four months, all should be numbered with the dead. This mortality would be no more awful than that which I have witnessed in the Crescent City."

It is interesting to note that Dr. Clapp pays the highest tribute to the Catholic priests of New Orleans for their work during the epidemics: "In the epidemic of 1832 I was the only Protestant clergyman that remained in the city, except the Reverend M. Hull, of the Episcopal church, who was confined to his house by a lingering consumption and unable to leave his room. This gentleman never left the city in sickly seasons, but fearlessly continued at his post, however great and alarming the mortality around him. So it was that in the first cholera I had no coadjutors but the Roman Catholic priests."

It is also interesting to note that Dr. Clapp speaks of his aversion for the Catholic religion at The time of his arrival in New Orleans. He soon changed his mind, for he found the priests to be cultured gentlemen some of whom where as broad as the good Presbyterian minister himself. It is interesting nowadays, in this time of religious hatreds, to read a memoir so intelligent, and so truly Christian in spirit as this one of Dr. Clapp's.

His name is still honored in New Orleans, by Catholic and Protestant alike.

His description of the yellow fever epidemics is particularly interesting in view of modern scientific knowledge. In the epidemics of his day, the fear of the unknown was added to the fear of the disease itself.

When it was discovered, in 1905, that the fever was caused by the sting of a mosquito, and by that alone, the city was able to protect itself. There have been no epidemics since that time.

Chapter V

A Little History in Street Names

The public library and Tulane University of New Orleans offer an interesting field for speculation in terms of street names - for in them the history and character of the city is written. Earlier we encountered names in the Vieux Carre. These names reflected the spirit of the founders; and as the city grew, and new streets came into being, new history was written. Let us now consider the names of some of these streets.

In naming the streets several systems were pursued. The French Creoles christened a number of streets after the favorite children of rich parents, while others were named after favorite concubines. Such names as Celeste, Suzette, Estelle, Annette and others were common. Some of these have changed into new titles, but many still remain.

The religious tendency of the people reflected itself in the religious names given many of the streets. Several hundred saints were so honored. Besides these, there were such street names as Conception, Religious, Nuns, Assumption, Ascension and so on.

Just about the time of the French Revolution, the Roman and Greek fashions were in vogue. The French imitated the ancient classics by assuming the Roman dress and names. The Creoles followed the French and all the names of antiquity were introduced into Louisiana and survive to this day. The streets found similar fate and were liberally christened from pagan mythology.

Next came the Napoleonic Wars with intense enthusiasm over the victories of the Corsicans. A general in Napoleons army who settled in Louisiana, went so far as to name the whole upper portion of the city in honor of the little Emperor. Napoleon Avenue, Jena Street and Austerlitz Street are samples which survive to this day.

In addition came the names and titles of early Louisiana planters, such as Montegut, Clouet, Marigny, Delord, the early governors of Louisiana, mayors of New Orleans and distinguished citizens.

The French are not so matter of fact as the Anglo-Saxons. For instance, no Anglo-Saxon would ever think of naming a street Goodchildren Street, rue Des Bons Enfants, or Love Street, rue d l' Amour, Madman's Street, Mystery Street or Piety Street.

Even when a person is acquainted with the names of New Orleans' streets, the problem is to know how to pronounce and spell them - because they are seldom pronounced as they would seem to be. For instance Tchoupitoulas - pronounced Chopitoulas - and Carondelet are examples by which foreigners are detected. No person is ever recognized as a true Orleanian until he can pronounce and spell these names correctly. A serious charge made against an Auditor of the State, that he spelled Carondelet, Kerionderlet aroused so much indignation of the population, they could never forgive this mistake.

A visiting scholar to New Orleans would most likely question the seemingly mispronunciation. In an effort to relieve the people of New Orleans of any charge of ignorance, I shall try to explain.

The Greek names are pronounced in the French style. The street that the scholar would call Melpomene, of four syllables and with the last 'e' sounded, would be in French Melpomene, and is translated by the people of New Orleans into Melpomeen. So Calliope is Callioap; Terpsichore is Terpsikor; Euterpe, Euterp; and others in the same way. French pronunciation and spelling are preserved and have become current among English-speaking portions of the population.

The constant annexation to New Orleans of suburban villages and towns, with streets of the same name produces inconvenience to both strangers and natives. There is a duplicate to many names and sometimes four or five streets bearing the same name.

Here are some of the street names which are somewhat unusual: Coliseum, Benifit, Cotton Press (now Press), Desire - which is next to Nun Street - Exchange Passage, Frenchmen,

Senius, Grand Route St. John, Numonitz, Industry, Independence, Lower Line, Upper Line, Mystery, Magazine, Perdido, Piety, Pleasure, Virtue, Mandolin, Rabbit, Poet, Plum, Socrates, Salomon, Shakespeare, Conti (pronounced Contie) Tonti pronounced TonTee, Julia Street - the old guide books tell us - was named for a free woman of color. It was the most fashionable residential street in the section. Now it is in the wholesale district, but it's still Julia Street. Who was Julia? I do not know. But if the reader is interested in more detail on some of the fascinating people and buildings that make up the story of New Orleans; let him(her) walk with me among these beautiful old buildings in the French Quarter, where pirates, aristocrats and vendors walked-generations ago. We shall start our walk at the lower/northern part of the Quarter and work our way toward Canal Street, the dividing line between North and south.

Let us begin at...

1300 Decatur Old U.S. Mint was built on the site of Fort St. Charles in 1815. It operated from 1838 to 1862 and, after the Civil War, from 1879 to 1910. It has just been restored and now houses the Geneological Research Library and Historic Center as well as a Mardi Gras Exhibition and a U.S. Jazz exhibit.

The Street Car Named Desire is restoredd to its original 1906 style. In the 1920's the streetcars were modernized to look like the ones still running on St. Charles Avenue. On Saturdays and Sundays a public flea market is held under the shadow of the mint.

800,900, 1000 Decatur, The French Market was actually the market place of the Choctaw Indians who travelled to the river bank to display their wares. Early German farmers came by boat to sell produce and dairy products here. The Spanish put up a market building in 1771, but a hurricane destroyed it in 1812. The next year it was replaced by the building you see closest to Jackson Square, The Butcher'Hall. In 1822 the vegetable market was built and the third building, in 1872. A fourth building was just added in 1975, when the entire market underwent an extensive restoration (which preserved and modernized the interiors of the buildings, but also, greatly changed the look, feeling and purpose of the whole Market.

700 Decatur Moon Walk, gives an excellent view of the Mississippi. Try to picture the huge sailing ships from far away ports and myriad of small boats which must have dotted the river. Later, paddlewheeler's (like those you can still see) lined the bank, and the wharfs were busy with cargo and passengers.

The present scene is impressive, too. One of the largest ports in North America! The Greater New Orleans Bridge, on the right was built in 1958.

Turning, around, you see the center of all that was important to New Orleans. It was in this Square that the Flags of six governments were raised as the city changed hands. Citizens gathered here for celebration, meetings and ceremonies. All the notables and immigrants who shaped New Orleans'history were first received in Jackson Square.

1114 Chartres, Old Ursuline Convent is one of the oldest buildings in the Mississippi Valley. It was built for the Sisters of St. Ursula, soon after they arrived from France in 1727. From here they operated Louisiana's first Catholic, Negro and Indian schools and first orphanage. They moved in 1824 and from 1831 the State Legislature occupied the building. It then became the Archbishop's Palace until 1899.

711 Chartres, St. Louis Cathedral. Bienville built a small church here that was destroyed by a hurricane in 1722. Then, another church was built of brick which lasted until the 1788 fire. Soon after, the wealthy Don Almonaster started the present Basilica and it was designated a cathedral in 1793. The original Spanish style had just two steeples, which were bell shaped. A central bell shaped steeple was added in 1820. Then, in 1851, the church was completely rebuilt to appear more French as you see it today.

709 Chartres The First Cabildo was first built here in 1769by O'Reilly on the site of old French buildings, it burned in 1788. Its replacement, begun by Don Andres Almonaster y Roxas, burned in 1794. Starting the present building 1795, he incororated the remains of the previous Cabildos (made of bricks of river mud and sand) In 1803, the Louisiana Purchase was signed here and the building became the city hall until 1853. Pierre Lafitte was jailed here in 1814 and Lafayette was royally housed here in 1825. The building is now a state museum offering fascinating display of New Orleans history.

538 Chartres, **Fire of 1788,**which destroyed 856 buildings, started in a home on this site, when curtains blew intogood Friday religious candlles. Most of the French buildings were lost and soon were replaced by new spanish architecture. Some contend that the fire actually started across the street **619 Chartres, Bosque House.** This unusual Spanish home was built in 1795 by Bartholome bosque.

601 St Louis, Louis Exchange Hotel stood proudly along this block completed in 1840. It was a grand hotel where wealthy planters stayed when they came to New orleans from the plantations. The bar was always crowded with men buying and selling slaves or merchandise on the auction block. Magnificent balls were held on the marble floor under the huge domed ceiling of the ballroom. Later, the hotel stood empty for many years, and, despite the cries to save it, it was torn down in 1917.

500 Chartres, Napoleon House was built in 1797 by Mayor Girod, who offered it to Napoleon, when he was exiled on Elba. But, Napoleon went on to Waterloo instead of New Orleans. Then, when exiled again,Girod hired Jean Lafitte's brother (alias Dominique You) to go to St. Helena in a specially built racing boat and kidnap the willing Napoleon, but the little emperor died before this could all take place.

437 Royal, The Cocktail was invented here, in Antoine Peychaud's apothecary (opened in 1800) He served his fellow

Masonic Lodge members special drinks made with his own blend of bitters.

713 St. Louis, Antoines, The oldest restaurant in New Orleans, was started by Antoine Alciatore in 1840 and is today, still operated by his family. He first opened his restaurant as a "pension" or boarding house. In 1870, he moved his very popular kitchen into this 1850's building (which now encompasses 5 buildings including 14 dining rooms)

533 royal, Merieult House was built by wealthy Jean Francois Merieult in 1792. The doorways were brick arches originally, but remodeled to their present in the 1830's. The building houses the Historic New Orleans Collection, which features historical exhibits of photos, maps, paintings and documents. Behind the housse is another home (which can be toured). It is prserved just as it was earlier in this century, when it was the elegant and social home of a prominent New Orleans couple.

621 Royal, Zachary taylor, 12th president of the U.S. lived in this lovely old home in 1840. The house dates from about 1825.

Pirates'Alley is said to have been the haunt of pirates and smugglers, before the street was actually cut in 1831.

1140 Royal, The Haunted House claims one of t he saddest histories in the old city. Louis Barthelemy deMcCarthy built the house and gave it, in 1831, to his daughter, Delphine LaLaurie. She held many grand parties here, but gossip grew about the suffering and possible suicide of her slaves. One night, in 1834, the house caught fire and as neighbors entered to put it out, they found 7 starving and tortured slaves, chained in agony. The LaLauries fled from the city as horrified neighbors wrecked the house in rage. The house Was later restored but many say the tormented souls of her unhappy servants still haunt it.

1315 Royal, Gauche House. This "Italianate Villa" was built in 1856 by John Gauche, who had the cast iron balconies made in Saarbruchen, Germany.

Notice lovely Esplanade Street, one of the prettiest in the city. Royal Street was the first in the Vieux Carre to be paved (in1823, with stone blocks brought over as ballast on European sailing ships).

717 Orleans, Orleans Ballroom. \Built in 1817 by John Doors, as the Salle d'Orleans, the building hosted the most fashionable, "high class" balls, including one held for Lafayette in 1825. In 1838 the character changed and the "Quadroon Balls" began. Mothers would preseent their beautiful mulatto daughters for the aristocratic white creoles to choose and "set up" as concubines. Many duels were fought in St. Anthony's Garden(which you can see at the end of the street) for the honor of these mistresses. In 1873, Thomy Lafon a "free man of color" bought the building for the Negro Sisters of the Holy Family as a chapel for their orphanage.

726 St. Peter, Preservation Hall. By day, an intriguing look through the omate iron gate to the lush, quiet courtyard behind the mysterious old building. By night, the hall is packed with enthusiasts clapping to traditional jazz.

624 Bourbon, Fortin House. This large home was built in 1834 by a young doctor for his bride. As you walk through the lovely patio, notice that neighboring courtyards were often connected by small doorways.

541 Bourbon, The French Opera House stood on this site from 1859 until it burned in 1919. Considered by many to be the cultural "heart of New Orleans", it was the setting for Mardi Gras balls, receptions for debutantes and grand opera productions. New orleans was proud of its famous operas and the galleries were always jammed for the colorful productions--an evening of music sometimes lasting a full six hours. Surrounding the opera house were all the shops related to its carnival balls and grand opera productions; wig makers, tailors, mask makers, etc. Notice that the street is wider where the carriages stopped to let off their elegant passengers.

430 Dauphine, Pierre Cottage a Frenchman, Pierre Malreaux, bought this property from the Spanish government in 1780 and soon built this charming cottage, making the bricks in the courtyard and using Lake Pontchartrain shells in the mortar. Only partially damaged in the 1788 fire, it is one of the oldest Bordeaux brick between post) cottages remaining.

As you face the house, look up to your left at the faded letters on the tall corner building. Throughout the Vieux Carre, you will see signs left from the many years through which these old buildings have stood.

400 Bourbon, Old Absinthe Bar is proud of the original marble bar and absinthe drip fountains, rescued from the old Absinthe House when prohibition officers closed it in the '20's

327 Bourbon, Judah P. Benjamin, secretary of state for the Confederacy, lived in this house, built, with its distinctive ironwork, in 1834.

238 Bourbon, Old Absinthe House was built in 1806 by two Spaniards and is still owned by their descendants in Spain Customers here sipped absinthe, a strong liqueur made from wormwood and now outlawed. This is one of the places where Andrew Jackson is said to have met with the Lafitte brothers to plan the defense of New Orleans.

We are now about two blocks north of Canal street having identified one fourth of an area that is rich in the history and character of the City. The remaing seventy five per cent, I can assure you, will prove equally as interesting.

But here is where I leave you. You are now on your own, Good luck.

Chapter VI

Gamblers - River and Land

Gambling on the river was recognized as an established institution. Steamboat captains, as a rule, considered it bad luck to leave a dock without a gambler on board, and no attempt was made to hinder him in his operation of fleecing the passengers. From about 1835 until the Civil War he was in his heyday. It is estimated that from six hundred to eight hundred men worked the big boats, called "floating palaces", between New Orleans and St. Louis. Most contemporary writers agree that as a class he was the best-dressed man in the United States with his black soft hat, black broadcloth coat and trousers, black high-heeled boots, black tie, and white shirt. The embellishment of these basic garments evoked a more detailed description by one writer:

"The white shirt was cut low in the neck, with a loose collar and a bosom frilled and frizzled and only partly concealed by a fancy vest, fastened with pearl, gold, or diamond buttons. At least three diamond rings on his smooth fingers, and another stone, known as a "headlight" as large as he could afford, enhanced the white shirt. In a pocket of the fancy vest was his watch, usually big and gold, set in precious gems. A long gold chain was attached to the watch then looped about his neck and dropped across his shirt-front."

Jimmy Fitzgerald, a New Orleans sharper who - it is said - made and lost a fortune playing poker and faro on the river in the 1840s was perhaps the best dressed gambler of his time. He sent to Paris for his boots, had four overcoats and many expensive suits. When he came aboard a steamboat he was followed by three slaves bearing his trunks. He was a reckless and spectacular player, and what he made on the river he lost in gambling houses on land. He was known to "call the turn" at faro. He was frequently wrong and consequently loose his wardrobe, diamonds and Negroes.

But two or three weeks after such luck he invariably appeared on the steamboats as flush and resplendent as ever, complaining because his new boots had not yet arrived from Paris. If Fitzgerald had any peers as a fancy dresser they were probably Gib Cohern, and Jim NcLane, whose mother gave him ten thousand dollars a year to stay away from home; Tom Mackey, who also bought Paris boots; Star Davis, from whom a famous race horse was named and who finally became a heavy drinker and was killed in a fall down a flight of stairs in a St. Louis hotel; and Napoleon Bonaparte White, better known as Paley White, came to New Orleans from Washington as a boy, about 1840, and became a gambler after a brief try at steamboat engineering. After the Civil War he married and settled in New Orleans where he operated a gambling-house on St. Charles Avenue in partnership with Sam Williams. The business prospered, but most of Palely's money was spent trying to save his two sons Benny and Jimmy, who were described by the New Orleans Picayune as "desperate characters who made the old man's life a burden to him". Benny died of alcoholism in jail while awaiting trial for a shooting and Jimmy was last heard of in California, where he had killed two men, one of them in a fight over a bottle of wine. In 1889, broke and upset by a new anti-gambling law, Paley borrowed a few dollars from a Royal Street bartender and bought a pistol and an ounce of sulphate of morphine. Then he called all of his friends and told them good-bye, saying he was gong home to kill himself, which he did.

Another noted fashion-plate of the decade preceding the Civil War was Colonel Charles Starr, known among gamblers as the biggest liar on the river. To hear him tell it he owned at least half of the plantations on the Mississippi from New Orleans to St. Louis. He gambled only because he was bored by his vast holdings and uncountable wealth. He hired Negroes to meet whatever steamboat he was traveling on at various landings and hail him as "Massa Kunnel" representing themselves as overseers on his broad holdings and asking his instructions on various matters. Starr was very popular despite his tendency to bragg. Many of the anecdotes in which he figured are still used by after-dinner speakers but without acknowledgment to Starr.

Colonel Starr accumulated a sizable fortune as a river-boat gambler, but later went broke trying to break the faro banks in New Orleans and St. Louis. When he was finally down and out with no resources at all, he entered a New Orleans restaurant where he had been a frequent and welcome guest in the days of his prosperity, and ordered an elaborate meal. The manager insisted he pay in advance. Without a word, the Colonel left the place. He returned in an hour with five dollars for which he had pawned his overcoat, and ordered the best meal obtainable for that amount. When he was served he deliberately and very carefully turned every dish upside down on the table. Then he walked out. That very night he died. Many of these elegantly attired slickers were crooked, and were known as "sure-thing players". They were experts at palming cards and dealing from the bottom of the deck. They knew how to use such cheating devices as vest, table sleeve and belt hold outs and poker rings and other devices known in the trade as "advantage tools".

All of these so called "advantage tools" were sold by dealers in New York and Chicago, who would send salesmen to demonstrate samples and take orders from the gamblers. Most of the big money made on steamboats were made with marked cards or "readers" which were played beforehand with the bartender and sent to the gamblers' table when new or fresh decks were called for. Sometimes instead of using marked, "stripped decks" were used. On a stripped deck, a fraction of an inch (never more than 1/32) was cut from the edges of all but three or four of the highest card with a tool called a "stripper plate". The fact that these few cards being insignificantly larger, went unnoticed, but the expert manipulator in shuffling, dealing or cutting, could place them where ever he wished. "The benefit of these cards", said a dealer's catalog, "can only be estimated in one way and that is: how much money has your opponent got: For you are certain to get it; whether it's $10 or $10,000".

Not all river gamblers were crooked. Of the few old timers known as "square shooters" who depended entirely upon their luck and skill, the most celebrated were Dick Hargraves, John Powell, and Major George M. White. White followed for sixty-two years, gambling as a profession. It is said that he won and lost a dozen fortunes. He began his career in New Orleans in 1825, when he was twenty years old and dealt his last card in 1887. He died in San Francisco in 1900 at the age of ninety-five.

Hargraves, as the saying goes, "was a slim dapper man with suave and polished manner". He came to New Orleans from England about 1840, when he was sixteen, and became a bartender, but turned to gambling when he won thirty thousand dollars in a poker game with a sugar-planter named Duprey.

Hargraves worked the river steamboats for some ten years with great success. At one time he was said to be worth two million dollars. At the height of his prosperity he got involved in an affair with the wife of a New Orleans banker. He killed the banker in a duel. Then the brother of the wife announced that he would kill Hargraves on sight. They met in a resort at "Natchez - under the Hill", said to be one of the famous hell-holes of the Mississippi, Hargraves killed the brother in a desperate fight. When he returned to New Orleans the wife of the banker stabbed him and committed suicide. Hargraves recovered, married a girl whom he had rescued from a fire in Mobile, joined a filibusting expedition to Cuba. When the Civil War began he became a major in the Union Army. Soon after the war ended he went to Denver, where he died of tuberculosis during the early 1880s.

John Powell was from Missouri but lived in New Orleans most of the time he was ashore. He was thought of as the most distinguished, well-educated, and always richly dressed without the vulgar flashiness of some of his contemparies. His manners left nothing to be desired. His personality and charm made him welcome in the best of society. He was a friend of Andrew Jackson and most of the important Louisiana politicians who often sought his counsel. His greatest success came as a gambler from about 1845 to 1858. He was considered the most daring and expert poker player on the river with the exception of Hargraves. He was probably the most consistent winner and richest of all "square" gamblers who worked the steamboats. When he was fifty years old, in 1858 Powell owned a theater and other property in New Orleans.

He owned a hundred-thousand-dollar farm stocked with fine horses and slaves in Tennessee, and large real estate holdings in

St. Louis. His friend tried to get him to retire, but he said gambling was in his blood and that he would gamble until he died.

Powell's luck on the river however ended in 1858. In the Summer of that year he was one of the players in a famous poker game aboard the steamer Atlantic with two other professional "square players" and Jules Devereaux, a rich Louisiana planter. Within an hour after play had begun there was thirty-seven thousand dollars in gold in sight on the table, and on the first hand dealt, Powell is said to have won eight thousand dollars. The game continued without intermission for three days, during which time the four men, drinking only the finest wines, ran up a bar bill of $791.50. Devereaux's losses are said to have been approximately a hundred thousand dollars of which Powell won slightly more than half. A few months later Powell played a two-handed game of poker with a young English tourist and won eight thousand dollars and all of his luggage. Next morning after breakfast the Englishman shook hands with most of the passengers and then put a pistol to his head and blew his brains out. Powell sent the young man's money and luggage to his relatives in England and retired from gambling for a year. But when he returned to the steamboat both his luck and skill were gone. He is said never to have won another pot after his tragic win over the Englishman. Within another year he had lost all his property and was a shabby desperate man. When the Civil War began he went to Seattle, where he died in poverty in 1870.

Almost every known game of chance was played on the steamboat, but the most popular were poker, faro, twenty-one, seven-up, three-card Monte, and the shell game. Canada Bill and George Deval worked the steamboats together for many prosperous years, as Monte operators, but lost all their earnings playing faro on land. About 1850 they formed a partnership with two other gamblers, Tom Brown and Holly Chappell, and the four operated successfully. When they decided to split up each man's share it was about two hundred thousand dollars. These four "sure-thing" slickers had a free Negro servant called Pinch, whom Deval had found shining shoes in a steamboat barbershop and had taken a fancy to. His real name was Pinckney Benton

Stewart Pinchback and he was born in Macon, Georgia in 1837. Deval taught Pinch some of the tricks of the trade. While Deval and his partners were fleecing the white folks in the saloon with Monte and poker, Pinch was on deck fleecing the Negroes. In later years Pinch continued to do well for himself. He quit the river when the Civil War began and in 1862 ran the Confederate blockade at Yazoo City and reached New Orleans soon after the capture of the City by Farrayut. Pinch soon rose to a high position among the Negroes. After the war he organized the Fourth Ward Republican Club and became a member of his party's State Committee. In 1868 he was elected to the State Senate and in 1871 was chosen Lieutenant Governor from December 9, 1872 to January 13, 1873. He was elected in 1873 to the U.S. Senate. The Senate, however, after three years of debate refused to seat him.

While he was occupying the gubernatorial chair, Pinchback repaid, in some measure, the man who had given him a start in life, so to speak. As the story goes, Deval had won eight hundred dollars from one of the police commissioners of New Orleans at Monte on the river. And when he arrived in the city a few days later he was summoned at once to police headquarters by the Chief of Police who said he had been ordered to run the gambler out of town. Deval immediately went over to the Executive Mansion where he saw his old boy Pinch for the first time in about fifteen years. Pinch, the Governor, aroused his servants, an elaborate supper was served and he and Deval played seven-up until morning. At dawn Pinchback escorted the gambler to the door and said: "Go to bed, George, and don't give yourself any uneasiness. I'll take care of that Police Commissioner". Deval was an important person among the so called "sure-thing" players of the Mississippi. He began gambling professionally at fifteen and within a year he was quite a cheat with a bank roll of about three thousand dollars, which in those days was a lot of money for a sixteen-year-old boy to possess. While at the end of some fifty years of gambling he had very little money to show. Those who knew him well all agree that at least two million dollars passed through his hands, most going to faro banks in St. Louis, New Orleans and Chicago.

With the exception of Canada Bill Jones, Deval was probably the most skillful Monte and poker player who ever fleeced the suckers of the steamboats.

Chapter VII

Old Spain Remembered

Papa John, an Italian, lived in a one room house near the boarding house on Albonia Plantation. The house was provided for single men rent free, in exchange for their labor for which they received a maximum of eighty cents a sixteen-hour day. A home-made bed, with a Spanish-moss mattress, one chair, and a kerosene lamp came with the house. No stove. Cooking was done in the fireplace.

My folks ran the boarding house next door. Papa John became my friend. His sole possession was a nanny goat that produced the milk from which cheese was made to sprinkle over the delicious spaghetti he would cook over the fireplace.

One day he would leave the plantation and move to Port Arthur, Texas to live with his daughter Annie. Then, he said the goat would be mine.

Papa John lived in New Orleans with his wife and daughter Annie until Annie was a teenager. When his wife died he sent Annie to live with his sister in Port Arthur and he came to the plantation. I was a frequent visitor at Papa John's for two reasons, the spaghetti, and the stories he told.

According to Papa John this story originated with his great grandmother who was part Spanish, living in New Orleans when the city was a colony of Spain. Papa John's grandmother would often tell her daughter, who was Papa John's mother, "how things used to be". She would close her eyes and say, with a sigh, "Ah, it was just like a part of Old Spain."

She remembered: it's a Sunday morning in the Spring. Looking toward the convent near the river bank you see black-robed nuns saying their beads in a high-walled garden. You can hear the sleeping sound of childrens' voices reciting verses together; the cooing of pigeons under the eaves.

Outside the grilled gateway, Negro slaves pass by in the

narrow street on their way to market, bearing baskets of purple figs upon their head. Women in silk with downcast eyes walk under the sycamores on their way to the church of San Luis. On the flat roof of the Cabildo next door, yucca is growing in many squat jars, the leaves dark and jagged.

From within the church comes the sound of a priest's voice chanting; and through the arched doorway see his gestures as he says the mass.

Twilight comes and lanterns are lit in the town. The twanging of guitars comes from the cabarets; a man's voice is heard singing a song of the tonos.

Before long the zoom-zoom of the tom-toms is heard in Congo Square, where the Negroes dance - a dance as old as Africa itself.

And later the sound of singing in the street as the revelers are returning home. Then quiet again, and the voice of the watchman crying out the hours, and calling the message that all us well.

Yes, the old lady would say, this is how it was ......

On weekdays you could hear the hammer on anvil as the slaves beat out the iron work for a grill above the door of the Cabildo. The sound of mallet strokes is heard in Royal Street, where mansions are rising to replace wooden houses destroyed by fire. Brick walls are going up. Within the courtyards is a smell of damp plaster, and cedar and cypress wood.

But muffled screams of agony are coming from the Calabozo as Temba the Hunter is stretched upon the rack in an effort to make him confess the murder of his master. Spanish authorities, wearing brocade and velvet, sit in the council chamber waiting for the slaves to tell what he knows. Pain will break his spirit before long. When he confesses, there will be more torture, and at last his head will be chopped off and stuck up on a pole at the Tchoupitoulas Street Gate.

Near by in the Place d'Armes, Creole children crowd around a puppet show - a toy which has come from Spain for their amusement. A priest comes by and pat the children on their head: "Have fun my chickens". He always called the little children his chickens.

He smiles, but his heart is heavy. He is on his way to tell a quadroon mother that her daughter cannot be buried from the church. She has committed suicide - a sin against the Holy Ghost - because her lover has taken a younger mistress. She was a pretty wench too, and nearly white. What a fool! As if there were not many men in the world. She lies dead today, yet just last night she danced at the quadroon ball.

From the Calabozo the cries of Temba can be heard no longer. Perhaps it was like this:

Chapter VIII

A Ghastly Man

During the last decade of this twentieth century there has been a rising tide of man's inhumanity to man - manifesting itself here in the United States through acts of violent crimes. Many of the victims include innocent children murdered by their own parents. Many have shuddered at the horror of these crimes. But in the early history of this country there are incidents which rival any imaginable violence and cruelty anywhere on earth. One such incident follows:

But first it's necessary to explain the military situation in Louisiana under the governship of Kelerec in New Orleans. It seems a wholesale military execution took place. Money was scarce, the soldiers were not paid and fed adequately. As a consequence there were frequent deserters. The English Army welcomed them with open arms. The men deserted in such large numbers that New Orleans had to depend upon Swiss Mercenary troops for protection. The Swiss headquartered on Ship Island, lying in the Gulf of Mexico not far from the mouth of the Mississippi River. Their commander was a Frenchman named Duroux. I was unable to find a description of the man himself, but from what I've learned from documents of the time, he was a man of unusual meaningless cruelty. Being in charge of a large group of men he made himself a monarch. He made a private fortune from his Charcoal Kilns and the field under the tropical sun. He frequently used the whip on those whom he considered lazy or disobedient. Here is a chilling and gruesome plea of one man: Because I was unable to do the work assigned to me, I was brought to him (Duroux) for an explanation. I swore to him that I had done my best, but that my strength was insufficient for the labor imposed upon me. He set four men upon me. They threw me to the ground, stripped me naked. Duroux himself applied the whip. He struck me again and again until I lost consciousness. One eye was put out by a blow from the butt of the whip.

He ordered the four men to take me far enough from his dwelling so that my cries would not disturb his rest at night. There I was bound to a tree. In my nakedness I was prey to the mosquitoes which settled upon me in swarms. I remained there for two days and two nights without food or water.

My brother, who had made some attempt to soften his heart, was tied naked to a tree near-by. In this position, standing with his back to the tree, and with his body exposed to the sun, he presented a pitiful sight. His body was covered with blood and was black with flies and mosquitoes. He was released at the end of thirty-six hours, but died the following day.

At times there have been as many as fourteen men, naked and tied to stakes in the sun on the beach. Duroux walked up and down before them, prodding them in the softer parts of their bodies with his sword, enough to draw blood.

The men were almost driven mad by these inhumane tortures. Some managed to escape to New Orleans from Ship Island. They appealed to Governor Kelerec showing their scars and telling their story. Kelerec listened then had them thrown in prison, declaring them to be mutinous. After all Duroux was an officer and must be upheld. Any way, historians tell us the Swiss were sent back to Ship Island loaded down with chains. What became of them afterward we have no way of knowing.

Duroux, now free from worry about reprimand from a superior officer, treated the Swiss more mercilessly than before. He invented new tortures for those who did not do enough work to please him. Men were burned and mutilated now for the least offense or no offense at all. The island became a veritable hell.

Duroux frequently went hunting on neighboring islands and it was a whim of his to be received in state when he returned. One day he returned at sunset and as his boat approached the beach the usual guard filed out with drums beating and flags wavering. But as he stepped ashore, the men opened fired on him. Duroux fell dead.

His body was thrown in to the Gulf of Mexico and then the armed guard went over the island liberating the prisoners. Some escaped and some were captured and court martialed by the Swiss regiment stationed in New Orleans under the command of

Kelerec. The deserters were condemned to death. The leader of the deserters was broken on the wheel. All of the others were nailed alive in coffins and sawed in two.

Chapter IX

Storyville

Professional historians, newspapers, preachers, libraries, tabloids, and natives generally referred to the New Orleans of the early 1800s through the 1920s as Storyville. The name was derived from Sidney Story, a city alderman who had introduced an ordinance designed to confine the red light district, prostitutes, and bordellos to a designated area in the city. Many were concerned that if prostitution was allowed to spread, dominating elements such as gangs, hoodlums, and the mafia would also spread.

In the foreword I said this book would be an informal, but not in-depth account of New Orleans, known as the wickedest city in the world. Well, it will be difficult to maintain that stance because Storyville has been well chronicled for many years in many respectable publications with a great deal of editorial fanfare. I shall do my best to minimize this detail without damaging the substance.

For ten years the Mafia, burglar gangs and hoodlums were monitoring elements in the New Orleans underworld. Prostitution continued to spread, especially in the French Quarter, where brothels began to appear on Villere, Marais, Robertson and Basin Streets which was north of Canal Street. Hundreds of prostitutes invade the city from all parts of the USA with their "Fancy men" and other male parasites. The authorities did little more than shifted most of the crib and sidewalk strumpets to the Franklin Street district, where they were not allowed to operate on the ground floors of all houses on Burgundy, Customhouse, Bienville, Dauphine, St. Louis, and Conti Streets. But most of them were two and three dollar houses and a few five-dollar houses.

The matter of tax assessments was the madam's least worry. The Mascot, a tabloid of the times, investigated the subject and found that many of the brothels were not assessed at all, especially such notorious dives as those run by Fanny Dicker, Frankie Belmont, Anne Deckert, and Annie Merrit, all on Customhouse Street. Annie Merrit, it was said, whose house was one of the worst in New Orleans, conducted her business in person until she was eighty years old. She smoked from twenty to thirty big black cigars every night.

The largest assessment found by the <u>Mascot's</u> investigation among the red lights was $1200.00 against Madge Leigh's house on Customhouse Street. Mamie Christine's place on the same street, a few years later, was assessed $300.00. Lulu White, across the street also was assessed $300.00. At the same time, Lulu owned $2,000.00 worth of furniture, a cut glass chandelier, team of fine horses, and diamonds worth more than $10,000.00, and a $7,400 pair of earrings. Despite all this Lulu died a pauper.

The most popular prostitute during the late 1800s was a striking strawberry blond named Abbie Reed. She operated out of one of the big brothels on Basin Street for a short while. She saved her money and went into business for herself. By 1892 she owned a place at No. 15 Burgundy Street near Canal St. and a large two-story house in Delord Street, which she had bought from Mayor Shakespeare and which she operated as a high class assignation house. Abbie Reed married Jules Kunemon, grandson of a wealthy planter of St. James Parish who had been educated in France and Germany, and whose mother lived in Paris.

Abbie left the Burgundy Street brothel in the hands of a housekeeper and went to live with Kunemon in the house on Delord Street. That's when the beginning of Abbie's trouble occurred. Kunemon was arrested in August 1893 for knocking her down in front of No. 15 Burgundy Street because she has rented the property to Gertrude Livingston, better known as Queen Girtie. The following September he cut her so severely with a paring knife she was hospitalized for a week. He told the police she angered him by her expressed desire to leave him and join Queen Girtie's staff. Abbie, however, had a different story. She said he attempted to kill her because she refused to sell all of her property and finance a business venture of his. When Abbie recovered from her injuries she hurriedly sold her two houses and went to Pensacola, Florida. She returned to New Orleans several years later (about 1904), calling herself Countess Kunemon, and went to work at Fanny Lambert's brothel on North Basin Street. The Sunday Sun announced that "her friends will be glad to hear that she us getting along so nicely".

Queen Girtie operated the Old Reed place on Burgundy Street for several years and "attracted a nice class of trade". despite the fact that her strumpets were quarrelsome, high-spirited and always fighting. Among themselves, one of these fights attracted much attention when Cecilo Torrence bit off on of Josie Vinton's fingers and was arrested. Helen Frank, one of the girls, testified that Queen Girtie would not let the bouncer stop the fight. Queen Girtie said "let then fight it out". The testimony of Helen at the trial caused Queen Girtie to kick her out in the streets. Only one of Girtie's girls was never involved in a fight. She was Josephine Clare, better known as Ice Box Josie. She was Girtie's principal attraction, advertised as the coldest strumpet in the red light district. A prize of $10.00 in trade was offered to the man who could arouse her. Many men accepted the challenge, but no record of any winners was ever seen.

It was about one hundred seventy five years after Bienville and his soldiers and convicts first set foot on the site of New Orleans before the authorities and the people realized that unless suppressive or regulatory measures were instituted the city would become one large brothel. One of the first to be heard on this ever increasing wave of vice that was sweeping the city was the Reverend E.A. Clay, Pastor of the Dryades German Methodist Church and President of the Society for the Prevention of Cruelty to Children. He was also active in rescuing young girls from the bordellos. On Sunday October 30, 1892, the Reverend Mr. Clay delivered a powerful sermon titled, "Some City Pitfalls and Snares", which helped a great deal to mobilize growing sentiment against this spread of prostitution. This is what he said:

"I am now going to speak to you, beloved, of the things

which I wish could be told without words. I am going to speak of those houses of darkness and death and blackness and despair, of those human slaughterhouses, of the gravest things of all the pitfalls in the way of virtue in this great city... There are over five hundred of these dark places scattered throughout this city from Carrollton to the barracks, and they run the gamut of condition from the palatial palaces of velvet and gilt down to the veriest stinking and reeking pesthole of foul hags and noisomeness. Fifteen hundred angels of death and damnation inhabit these places. They affect and imperil the virtue and honor of very girl in the city".

The police department attempted to establish some sort of control over prostitution in 1891 by proposing an ordinance that would provide for Compulsory Medical examination of "All women and girls notoriously abandoned to lewdness". Many city officials favored the law, but the idea was quickly dropped when the respectable ladies of New Orleans held mass meeting and denounced it as an insult to Southern womanhood; about a year later Alderman Harmon introduced an ordinance providing a segregated district and the insurance of licenses to prostitutes.

But this measure also hit the dust before the united opposition of clergymen and leading women of the city. Their argument was strangely enough, that such a law would recognize existence of vice in New Orleans. Several years later (around 1897) the City Council adopted the famous ordinance introduced by Alderman Sidney Story, a well known broker. Story had made an exhaustive study of the methods by which prostitutes was regulated in large cities in Europe. Story's plan would set aside an area in the French Quarter wherein prostitution was to be permitted but actually legalized. On February 8, 1897, and ordinance was introduced extending the limits of the district by including an area in the American section, but it was withdrawn because of protests from property owners of the Third District. On July 6, 1897, the original Story ordinance was amended and re-enacted to provide two distinct and unconnected segregated areas, one in the French Quarter and one above Canal Street as follows:

"Be It Ordained, by the Common Council of the City of New

Orleans, That Section 1, of Ordinance 13, 032 C.S., Be and the same is hereby amended as follows: From and after the first of October, 1897, it shall be unlawful for any prostitute or woman notoriously abandoned to lewdness, to occupy, inhabit, live or sleep in any house, room or closet, situated without the following limits, viz: From the south side of Customhouse Street to the north side of St. Louis Street, and from the lower or wood side of North Basin Street to the lower or wood side of Robertson Street [in the French Quarter]; 2nd:-And from the upper side of Perdido Street to the lower side of Gravier Street, and from the river side of Franklin Street to the lower or wood side of Locust Street [in the American section], provided that nothing herein shall be so construed as to authorize any lewd woman to occupy a house, room or closet in any portion of the city."

Additional sections provided a system of fines, ranging from five to twenty-five dollars, and imprisonment up to thirty days in default of payment, for violations of ordinance. It authorized the Mayor to close any house, wether within or without the segregated district which "may become dangerous to public morals", and require the occupants to move. If they failed to do so, the Mayor was given the power to place a policemen at the door to warn away all parties who shall undertake to enter".

The limits of the French Quarter district, as set forth in the amended ordinance, were the same as in the measure adopted on January 6, except that five blocks had been added by the inclusion of St. Louis Street.

For whatever reason, no prostitutes were permitted to establish themselves in the prescribed American section, and it was never used as a segregated district. As close as I can surmise, the decision to confine vice entirely within the French Quarter must have been made right after the passage of the amended act, however, in September 1897 - the Council adopted an ordinance providing that "on and from the first of January, 1898, it shall be unlawful...to open, operate or carry on any cabaret, concert-saloon or place where can can, clodiche or similar female dancing or sensational performances are shown, without the following limits, viz, from the lower side of Basin Street to the lower side of North Robertson Street, and from the south side of Customhouse Street to the north side of St. Louis Street". No provisions was made for the such sections of the city above Canal Street. The passage of these ordinances, and the intention of the city to enforce them, prompted the exodus of prostitutes who indignantly refused to be "herded like cattle". Property values and rentals in the proposed district sky-rocketed. The area finally designated as a quasi-legal red light district comprised five blocks on each of Customhouse, Bienville, Conti, and St. Louis Streets and three on each of North Basin, Treme (now Ninth, Liberty, Villere, Maris, North Franklin and North Robertson Streets. A total of thirty-eight blocks occupied by brothels and assignation houses, and by saloons, cabarets, and other enterprises which depended in vice for their prosperity. The removal of prostitutes to these streets was completed by 1898 and the new district was in operation fully under the sheltering shadow of the law, popularly known as Storyville - much to Alderman Story's disgust. The brothels were now safe from police interferences. Wise madams and crib girls made sure by continuing the customs of leaving quarters in the doorsteps.

Storyville soon had become the most celebrated red light district in the United States. Commanding the spotlight formerly shared by Congo Square and the Quadroon Balls. Visitors in previous days were escorted to Congo Square to see the dancing of slaves and to the Old Orleans Ballroom to watch the beautiful Quadroon Strut their stuff. Now they were taking to Storyville to see the plush and velvet parlors of sin dins where bawd shows. dancing in cabarets and to peek through shutters at the naked girls who sat patiently waiting for customers. A tour of the district would usually begin with a drink at the Arlington Annex, at Customhouse and North Basin Streets. this gateway to Storyville belongs to T.C. Anderson, saloon-keeper, political boss of the Fourth Ward, member of the legislature in two terms. Prior to 1908, owner of at least one of the prosperous brothels of North Basin Street, and said to have an interest in several others. Anderson also owned a restaurant and cabaret on Rampart Street, which he advertised as "The Real Thing", and two other saloons, the Stag on Gravier Street and the Arlington on Rampart. The

Annex was the most important place in Storyville. Decent politicians called it "Anderson's Town Hall". One official said "he was a discipled of the brand of politician who made New Orleans a shambles of corruption for almost a hundred years. He spent much time at the Annex giving out favors and making his wishes and comments known. So far as the red light district was concerned he was the law. This is what Will Irwin, writer on Collier's Weekly, February 29, 1908, had to say about Anderson:

"Briefly, here is the reason for Tom Anderson: With a little break here and there, New Orleans has been in the grip of a ring. No large city in the United States gets such poor returns for the public money expended as New Orleans. It is ill-paved, ill-policed, behind in municipal improvements; the public money is needed for a thousand and one sincere jobs. By the same token, no other city of the country runs vice of every kind so wide open. Tom Anderson has been a great help. Highly prosperous himself, he has not failed to divide up with the power which enabled him to prosper; and he has helped to make the saloon-keepers, the gamblers and the brothel-keepers generous. It was his goal to go to the legislature, and a grateful people, recognizing his services, rewarded him".

Billy Struve, a young police reporter on the <u>Item</u> first met Anderson about 1895. He helped him organize the Astoria Club and went to work regularly for Anderson in 1900, quitting his newspaper career. In 1907 Anderson gave him an interest in the business. With Billy's assistance Anderson's business affairs were very prosperous. He retained his political power and prestige as King of Storyville until the segregated district was abolished.

Anderson quit the saloon business soon afterwards and went into the oil business. Liberty Oil Company which he sold to Standard Oil. In 1928 after recovering from a serious illness, Anderson became very religious and often expressed the with that he had lived a different life. He married Gertrude Hoffmire sometimes known as Gertrude Dix, who for several years after about 1908 had operated the brothel at No. 209 North Basin Street, owned by Anderson, and the Arlington at 225 North Basin Street, in which Anderson had an interest. When

Anderson died on December 10, 1931, he left his estate some $120,000 to Gertrude, but the Will was contested by Mrs. Irene Delsa, widow of George Delsa, at one time manager of Anderson's Cabaret on Rampart Street. She claimed to be Anderson's daughter by his first wife, Emma Schwartz. When he married in 1879 or 1880, when he was a young bookkeeper of twenty-two. A settlement was effected whereby Mrs. Delsa was recognized as Anderson's daughter. She received a considerable part of the estate.

Billy Struve was still alive in 1934. He was much involved in the day to day operations of the Astoria Club on Rampart Street, where the author, a seventeen year old, with a system, was trying to learn the gambling business.

When the strumpets were ordered to move to Storyville, the police made no attempt to separate the races except to forbid white and black women to live in the same house; they did, however, occupy adjoining premises. During the twenty years of the red light district there was of course much mingling. Most of the cribs flimsy one-story shanties were in prices ranging from twenty-five cents to a dollar were on St. Louis and Franklin Streets with a few on Customhouse, Conti, and North Robertson: While the two and three dollar houses were located on Villere Marais, and North Liberty Street. The five-dollar houses were concentrated on North Basin Streets where business was conducted with elegance and ceremony. Rudeness and bad behavior on the part of the customers was frowned upon and drunken gentlemen were not admitted. When a man entered the parlor he was expected to buy a drink at once - at a considerable profit to the house of course - but the girls were not trotted out for inspection unless he so requested. The houses were expensively equipped with much plush, gilt and velvet. In many of them there were rooms with mirrored walls and ceilings which were available at special rates; and ballrooms with hardwood floors curtained platforms for indecent dancing. Other erotic displays which were given whenever the right money was in sight. In most of these exhibitions the ladies of the house participated, sometimes specialists were called in.

Some of the best brothels employed Orchestras to play each

night from about seven o'clock to closing (about dawn). Others relied on groups of itinerant musicians who appeared in Storyville playing in the streets and saloons for coins and drinks. A group of boys from twelve to fifteen calling themselves the Spasm Bond was one such group. They were the real creators of jazz - seven members plus the manager and organizer Harry Gregsin, who was the singer - he crooned songs of the day through a piece of gas pipe, because he could not afford a megaphone. the musicians were Emile LaComb, aka Stalebread Charley who played a fiddle made out of a cigar box; Willie Bussey aka Cajun, who played the harmonica; Charley Stein, who manipulated an old kettle, a cow bell, a gourd filled with pebbles and other traps, and in later life became a famous drummer; Chinee played the bull fiddle, a coffin-shaped contraption built by the boys; Warm Gravy; Emile Benrod, called Whiskey, and Frank Bussey, known as Monks. the three last named played whistle and various horns. Most of them home-made and each had at least three instruments, upon which he alternated. Cajun, Bussey and Stalebread Charley could play tunes upon the fiddle and harmonica, and others contributed whatever sounds chanced to come from their instruments.

The Spasm Band first appeared in New Orleans around 1895, playing in front of theaters and in saloons and brothels with a few engagements at West End Grand Opera House. They were advertised as "The Razz Dazzy Spasm Band".

Their big moment was when they serenaded Sarah Bernhardt, who expressed delight and gave then each a gift. Around 1900 Jack Robinson, owner of the Haymarket dance-hall on Customhouse Street between Dauphine and Bourbon, hired a band of experienced adult musicians, who imitated the Spasm Band, even used their billing - Razz Dazzy Jazzy Band.

The carrying on and doings of the New Orleans strumpets were faithfully reported for some thirty years in half a dozen publications with much additional fanfares. The best-known of these were the Mascot, the Sunday Sun and the Blue Book. The Mascot issued every Saturday at five cents a copy, was about the size of the present day tabloid, with five to six pages. The Mascot, for about ten years was weekly with liberal tendencies.

It published sensational accounts of crime and scandal in the manner of the Police Gazette, but the editorial writer's comments were clear. In 1890 the Mascot began to devote a lot of space to the activities of the red light district. In 1894 it established a column called "Society" in which were published personal items about the prostitutes. The following sample is from various issues of 1894 and 1895:

"Madame Julia Dean has received a draft of recruits, and the fair Julia is bragging loudly of her importation. She seems to forget that the ladies played a star engagement here last Winter at Mme. Haley's, and they all carry their diplomas with them.

Several amateurs have been enjoying quite a good time of late in the residence at the rear of a grocery store on Derbigny Street.

The bewitching Miss Ollie Martinez has become so thoroughly domesticated of late that her name is becoming missed from the society columns.

It is safe to say that Mrs. [Madeleine] Theurer can brag of more innocent young girls having been ruined in her house than there were in any other six houses in the city."

The personal items and news accounts of the Mascot however were models of propriety and choice language compared with those of the Sunday Sun, an out and out scandal sheet. it was a bit smaller than the Mascot, with never more than four pages, and appeared weekly at newsstands and in saloons every Saturday at five cents. The front page was usually devoted to an account of a murder, a divorce case, or other scandal, and the story was very plainly written, usually under such headline as this:

Wife of ... commits herself in a most notorious, lewd and outrageous manner.
COMMITS ADULTERY
With a person known as ... who openly
Boasts that she is his woman.

The inside pages were filled with similar stories and with advertisements of saloons, quack doctors, pool-rooms, shyster lawyers, restaurants, cabarets, and assignation houses which made these announcements in this manner:

ELEGANTLY FURNISHED
ROOMS
1320 Conti Street ...Corner Liberty.
New Orleans, LA
MISS MAY EVANS

The feature accounted for the success of the <u>Sun</u> was a column headed "Scarlet World" and filled with frank comments on the doings of the harlots. These excerpts are good examples of the <u>Sunday Sun's</u> journalistic style and of its content:

"Nina Jackson who keeps the swell mansion, 1559 Customhouse Street, and who is herself one of the holiest girls in the bunch, has gotten rid of those two tid-bits, May and Mamie, and in their stead she has two of the finest and most-charming ladies to be found anywhere. Queen Emmette, known as the Diamond Tooth, is one of the girls, and Etta Ross is the other.

Nettie Garbright, who for a number of years kept a sporting house at No. 139 Customhouse Street, and retired to private life, is back on the turf again, comfortably situated at No. 1537 Customhouse Street.

Madge Lester has returned from a trip and is back in Jessie Brown's, 1542 Customhouse Street.

Boys, if you want to have a real jolly good time, don't overlook Miss Antonia Gonzales' establishment, for a visit to the village is incomplete without seeing Antonia and her array of beautiful young girls ...she keeps a swell house, where nothing but the best is kept.

The <u>Blue Book</u>, the most famous of all the red light publications, was the last of a series of books of the district. First came the <u>Green Book</u>, or <u>Gentlemen's Guide to New Orleans</u>, published in January 1895, in an edition of two thousand copies, which was quickly sold at twenty-five cents each. Next came the <u>Red Book</u>. It too was successful. The first issues of the <u>Blue Book</u> was about 1902 and supposed to have been financed by Tom Anderson. It appeared every year, contained from forty to fifty pages and was sold for twenty-five cents a copy in saloons, and by agents in hotels, railroad stations and steamboat landings. It was bound in blue paper with the words "Blue Book" printed in red. It contained a preface, a notice that "This book must not be mailed", and a complete list of "Late Arrivals", and a roster of the girls employed in the cabarets of the district. In the front and middle portion of the <u>Blue Book</u> were advertisements of saloons, lawyers, liquor-dealers, restaurants, cabarets, breweries, cigar and tobacco and other commodities. the last fifteen or twenty pages were the madams and street addresses in red. Here are a few of the best-known houses and madams with excerpts from their <u>Blue Book</u> advertisements.:

The Phoenix, 1547 Iberville Street, kept by Fanny Lambert. "Wine and beer house full of jolly an pretty Ladies".

Antonia P. Gonzales, corner Villere and Iberville Streets. "The above party has always been a headliner among those who keep first-class Octoroons. She also has the distinction of being the only Singer of Opera and Female Cornetist in the Tenderloin. She has had offers after offers to leave her present vocation and take to the stage, but her vast business has kept her among her friends. Any person out for fun among a lost of pretty Creole damsels, here is the place to have it".

The Firm, 224 North Villere Street. Kept by Miss Leslie. "The Firm is also noted for its selectness. You make no mistake in visiting The Firm. Everybody must be of some importance, otherwise he cannot gain admittance".

Eunice Deerings, corner Basin and Conti Streets. "Known as the idol of the society of club boys ...Aside from the grandeur of her establishment, she has a score of beautiful women".

Margaret Bradford, 1559 Iberville Street. "Pretty women, good time and sociability has been adopted as the counter sign of Miss Bradford's new and costly home".

Jessie Brown, 223 North Basin. "Don't be misled until you have seen Jessie Brown and her ladies".

The Cairo, 320 North Franklin. Kept by Snooks Randella. "Snooks has the distinction of keeping one of the liveliest and most elaborately furnished establishments in the city, where an array of beautiful women and good times reign supreme".

Martha Clark, 227 North Basin. "Her women are known for

their cleverness and beauty. Also, in being able to entertain the most fastidious of mankind".

The Club, 327 North Franklin. Kept by Maud Hartman.

"Come and join the club and meet the members".

Diana and Norma, 213-215 North Basin. "Their names have become known on both continents, because everything goes as it will, and those that cannot be satisfied there must surely be of a queer nature".

Gertrude Dix, 209 North Basin. "Miss Dix, while very young, is of a type that pleases most men of today - that witty, pretty and natty - a lady of fashion ... There are no words for her grandeur of feminine beauty and artistic settings".

Louis Dreyfus,1310 Conti Street. "She has some of the most beautiful and select girls in the district - one of whom is Chiquita, the Spanish Beauty".

Edna Hamilton, 1304 Conti Street. "as for women, she has an excellent array, who, aside from their beauty, are all of high class and culture".

The Studio, also known as the House of All Nations, 333 North Basin. Kept by Emma Johnson. "Everything goes here. Pleasure is the watchword. remember the name, Johnson's".

Grace Lloyd, 338 North Franklin. "A visit will teach you more than pen can describe".

Olga Lodi, the Italian Queen, 321 North Basin. "Aside from the magnificence of her home, she has a score of most handsome ladies, who are a jolly crowd to be among".

Countess Willie V. Piazza, 317 North Basin. "If you have the blue, the Countess and her girls can cure them. She has without a doubt, the most handsome and intelligent octoroons in the United States. You should see them; they are all entertainers".

May V. Spencer, 315 North Basin. "Miss Spencer, who is very young, is very charming, and above all things a favorite with the boys - what one might say, those of the clubs...You should see her girls".

Bertha Weinthal, 311 North Basin. "While still young of years, has nevertheless, proven herself a grand woman, has also made "good" as a conductor of a first-class establishment".

Minnie White, 221 North Basin. "She has surrounded herself with a bevy of charming girls, each one a star, who always willing to meet you halfway and make you feel you are welcome".

Josie Arlington, the most famous Madam of her time, operated the 225 North Basin Street bordello. She was to Storyville what Kate Townsend had been to the red light district of an earlier day. Josie's place was a five-dollar house. It was a four storied structure with bay windows in three sides and a cupola on the roof. Conservately painted outside but the inside was something else; plush velvet hanging oriental carpets, lace curtains, beveled mirrors, cut glass chandeliers, and Turkish corners crowded with bric-a-brac and valuable objects of many descriptions. Most of Josie's rival establishments housed less than six girls, but no fewer than ten exquisite strumpets trooped into the parlor at roll call at Arlington house. During the tourist and Mardi Gras seasons, this number was doubled. The Blue Book described the Arlington House as "absolutely and unquestionable the most decorative and costly fitted out sporting palace ever placed before the American public ... A palace fit for a king ...the most attractive ever seen in this or the old country...Many articles from various expositions will also been seen and curios galore", among the inanimate attractions of the bordello was a collection of steins which is said to have been really extraordinary. The entire collection was displayed on a shelf in the dining room, but since the house catered to many strangers, a heavy chain was passed through the handle of each stein and securely padlocked to a ring bolt sunk into the wall.

Josie's real name was Mary Deubler. She was born in New Orleans about 1864, of German parents, and was never married. When she was about seventeen years old, she fell in lobe with one Philip Lobrano, one obscure sporting man who was also known as Schwarz, and was his mistress for nine years, during which time she was a strumpet of various brothels on Customhouse and Basin Streets under the name of Josie Alton.

She didn't remain long in any one place, because of her hot temper and brawling and fighting. In 1886 she got into a terrible fight in Burgundy Street with a Negro prostitute, Beulah Ripley, in which she lost most of her hair, while Beulah staggered away from the combat with part of her lower lip an half an ear gone.

About 1888 Josie Arlington began calling herself Josie Lobrano, and opened a place of her own at No. 172 Customhouse Street, which she soon became known as one of the toughest houses in the city and the strumpets the most quarrelsome. On the profits of No. 172 Josie supported several members of her family and Lobrano, who lived in the house. Lobrano hated her relatives, often referring to then as "a flock of vultures". On November 2, 1890 during a fight in which Josie Arlington and all of her girls were involved, Lobrano shot her brother, Peter Deubler.

Lobrano was tried twice, and was acquitted at the second trial. After the shooting, Josie broke with her lover and changed her name to Lobrano d'Arlington, fired all of the fighting strumpets and announced that she would fill her house with gracious, amiable foreign girls who would be at home only to gentlemen of tastes and refinement. Early in 1895 a considerable stir was aroused in the red light district by this announcement in the <u>Mascot</u>.:

"Society is graced by the presence of a bona-fide baroness, direct from the court at St. Petersberg. The baroness is at presently residing incognito at the Chateau Lobrano d'Arlington, and is known as La Belle Stewart".

The baroness was exposed shortly as a hoochy-koochy dancer who had performed on the Midway at the Chicago World Fair. In spite of the exposure, the brothel was a success until Storyville was established, when she opened the Arlington where she became known as the snootiest madam in America.

She ran the place for ten years and amassed a fortune. She built a thirty-five thousand dollar house on Esplanade Street. She bought a plot of ground for two thousand dollars in Metarie Cemetery and erected an eight thousand dollar tomb of red marble on it. She began to be increasingly moody, and about 1909, it is said upon the advice of her friend, Tom Anderson and John T. Brady, she leased the Arlington to Anna Casey and retired to her house on Esplanade Street. There she lived with her niece, whom she had educated in a convent. On February

14, 1914 in her fiftieth year, she died and was buried the next day, after a quiet funeral. Her body was followed to the cemetery by a few carriages containing flowers, Sisters of Charity, priests, and a few male friends, among them according to the Item, Tom Anderson, John T. Brady, and Judge Richard Otero. A few months after Josie's death the city installed a red traffic light in the road along side the cemetery, and at night the glow struck the tomb in such a manner as to cause an illusion of a red light shining above the famous brothel's madams tomb. Crowds gathered each evening to watch the spectacle and it was one of the sights of the city until the red light was replaced with a white one. Josie's niece and Brady were married soon after the death of the madam, and about 1924 her bones were place in a receiving vault and the tomb sold.

On July 17, 1917 an ordinance was adopted establishing a special district for Negro prostitutes in the area bounded by the upper side of Perdido Street, and the lower side of Gravier, the river side of South Franklin, and the lower side of Locust Street. this act was to have become effective on August 15, but no effort was ever made to enforce it, for segregation vice in New Orleans had already been doomed by America's entrance into World War I.

After much back and forth bickering between the Army and Navy and Mayor Berman of New Orleans over the existence of Storyville, an ordinance was adopted that would make it unlawful beginning after midnight on November 12, 1917 to operate a brothel house anywhere in New Orleans. the exodus from Storyville had began two weeks before November 12th. As late as midnight of the 12th streams of strumpets could be seen with their servants laden with bundles leaving the area. During that afternoon the police informed the women that they could remain in Storyville, but they would be watched and arrested of they attempted to operated. On November 14, 1917, two days after the closing of the red light district, the Item announced that the police planned to round up the male parasites (fancy men) of Storyville and send them into the country to help the farmers. Nothing came of this idea. the prostitutes however, had simply moved from Storyville into various business and residential sections of New Orleans and were doing very well.

It can be concluded that Storyville was reasonably successful from the beginning, partly because public opinion favored such a district, partly because the police department increased in efficiency during the successive administrations of 1896 through 1920. The New Orleans experiment over a period of years proved that segregation with strict police supervision was the best method ever devised for the control of vice. Granted, street walkers, and occasionally an assignation house was discovered in forbidden territory, but the say when a family might suddenly find that the house next door has been transformed into a bordello ended with the Storyville Ordinance and didn't return until Storyville was abolished. Perhaps there was much truth in the remark of a high class bordello madam:

"The country club girls are ruining my business".

Chapter X

A Haven for Criminals

During the last three decades of the 19th Century, the City remained burdened with debts and corrupt politicians, despite the activities of reform committees which were organized in 1881 to suppress crime. Throughout these years the payrolls of all departments were padded with the names of hoodlums who were paid for their services a henchmen for the politicians.

The Mascot had this to say about these men on July 4, 1883: "Now adays, leaving Negroes out of the question, nine-tenths of the criminals arrested for drunkenness and ruffianly conduct are city employees. . . fully, a dozen of the "toughs" arraigned last week are drawing pay from the City".

Patrick Mealey was Commissioner of both the Department of Public Buildings and Commissioner of Police when two of his employees were charged with a stabbing of another employee who had been accused with stealing several hundred pairs of shoes. The Picayune, on October 3, 1885, ran these headlines regarding the incident:

> "Mealey's College of Crime
> Two of the Faculty Under Indictment
> In Criminal Court".

The Picayune went on to report a series of fatalities in which every man involved was prominent in state and city governments. The most sensational of these were the killing of three men and the wounding of eight others on December 14, 1883, in a pistol battle between groups of political rivals which included Robert Brewster, the Criminal Sheriff and James D. Houston, Tax Collector for the Upper District; Brewster was killed on January 12, 1885, when he and Houston tried to horsewhip the editor of the Mascot for publishing an article about Houston's brother, a judge; Patrick Mealy was killed on January 1, 1888 by John Gibson and Louis Clare, both notorious hoodlums and ward healers for the Democratic, machine". Captain Murphy, a workhouse keeper was killed by Patrick Ford and Policeman John Murphy. Clare and Gibson were sent to the penitentiary for life for killing Mealey. For killing Captain Murphy, John Murphy and Patrick Ford were hanged.

The police department was subject to little or no discipline. They reported for duty as they pleased, walked the streets in full uniform with prostitutes and engaged in drunkenness in public places. Many were open accomplices of burglars, pick pockets and crooked gamblers. A memorandum was sent to the Legislature in 1886 by a committee of one hundred denouncing the police force as "partisan and corrupt... largely contributing to the criminal ranks and largely recruiting from those ranks...Words cannot adequately describe the inefficiency of the preset police system. The memo caused a furor among the statesmen, but the members from New Orleans disposed of it in a manner which met approval of the entire Legislature - by issuing a statement accusing the committee of aping a previous committee which made similar charges in 1884. The <u>Picayune</u> published a statement under this head line, without comment,

"THE GALLED JADES WINCE!"

Many of the problems of the police were due to the large numbers of hoodlum favorites of the political leaders who were given jobs without regard to their record or qualifications, e.g. Lois Clare, who murdered Patrick Mealey, was appointed y Mayor Guillotte in July 1887. He was a well known ruffian and brawler and had been arrested thirty times in one year for fighting, drunkenness and stealing. Many of such characters were armed and clothed with the authority of policemen, but performed no regular police duties. They were paid from twenty to forty thousand dollars a year. They used their power to protect criminals, to escape arrest for their own criminal activities and of course to better serve their political masters as thugs and bullies. One of these thugs, T.J. Boasso, rose high in rank in the police force, but his career soon ending in a sensational scandal.

Boasso, the son of an Italian printer, entered politics in New Orleans as a ward-heeler for Guillotte and the state machine dominated by Governor Samuel D. McEnery. His first job was as keeper in the state insane asylum, but when Guillotte was elected Mayor, in April 1884, Boasso was appointed Acting Chief of Aids (as detectives were then called) although he was clearly not qualified for the job. During his brief time in office he was often in trouble with his superior officers because of his overbearing manner and his involvement with gamblers and con men. When one White Pine Russell, a bunko operator, was arrested for bilking a Colorado man of four hundred dollars, Boasso offered to return one hundred and fifty dollars if the complainant would not prosecute.

In spite of Boasso's alliance with the underworld, he continued to be one of Guilotte's intimate friends and advisors. In the summer of 1885, he went with the Mayor to a dinner party at the home of Ambrose Kuhn, a grocer, and met Kuhn's eighteen-year old twin daughters. According to the Times Picayune, Boasso "looked with lecherous eyes full on the twins", and chose Mary Catherine as his victim. He passed as a bachelor, although he had been married since 1881 (some four years earlier). He eloped with the girl the latter part of 1885. He showed her a bogus marriage certificate and she believed him when he said their signatures on the document would make them man and wife. When Kuhn learned the truth he rescued his daughter. She then went hunting for him with a revolver. She found him in front of a saloon on St. Anthony Street and shot him in the liver and the back. When re recovered he was tried, convicted of "forging and uttering a false marriage certificate" and sentenced to fourteen years in the state penitentiary. He served eight years and was pardoned by Governor Murphy J. Foster in 1894.

While the politicians and city officials were occupied with graft, murder and sectional rows, conditions in New Orleans, so far as crimes in general were concerned, were about as bad as in the days when the City was described as "a perfect hell on earth and the wickedest city in the world". Murder and robbery were common in the 1880's. Public places were so terrorized by hoodlums that they were unsafe for decent people and no respectable woman dared venture out at night without a strong escort. Most of these terrorizers were organized into bands and all carried revolvers, many had political connections which gave them a measure of immunity from punishment. They might go to jail occasionally, but the politicians soon got them out. Their liberty was jeopardized only when they committed murder and so came to the attention of the District Attorney. The newspapers were filled with the exploits of these hoodlums especially Tom Newhouse, Tug Wilson and Young Toramy McGittigan, who in 1886 at the age of eighteen, ended his brief and eventful career with a murder, for which he went to prison for life. Newhouse was a fireman until he killed his company commander and thereafter was never known to work although he was always on the payroll of some city department. He murdered a policeman in 1878, for which he was not punished, and in 1887 he killed George Maloney, a one-legged man. For this crime Newhouse went to prison for twenty (20) years.

Tug Wilson was, possibly, the most notorious and ferocious fighter in New Orleans after the Civil War. He was well known around the saloons, red light districts, bordellos and speakeasies from the early 1880's until his death in 1934. During Wilson's time hoodlums were the salt of the earth in New Orleans. In some six or eight years he was arrested more then one hundred times for fighting, drinking and gambling. While Tug Wilson was the perfect type of municipal employee, no record of him having worked for the city could be found.

Besides being overrun with hoodlums, New Orleans was a haven for well-organized gangs of burglars, pickpockets and sneak thieves. It was also the winter headquarters of many criminals of international notoriety; who lived openly at the best hotels, and went to the races and theaters. These seasonal visitors formed alliances and friendships with politicians and high officials of the city and state. Among the most distinguished of these visitors were Ned Lyons, Master Cracksman, and his wife, the celebrated Sophie Lyons-Levy; Jim

Kelly, a hotel thief better known as the Artful Dodger; John Larney, a pickpocket who was called Mollie Matches because he had once made a big killing in New York while disguised as a match girl; Big Tom Bigelow, a noted burglar who died at the St. Charles Hotel in November 1886 while stopping there with Little Louise Gordon, a shoplifter and sneak; Little Dave Cummings and Billy Forrester who robbed a Canal Street jeweler of $83,000 and a bank in the French Quarter of $65,000 and thereafter spent their vacations elsewhere; Red Leary, Jack Cannon; Paddy Guerin, Jimmy Carrolls, Dutch Fuddy Watson, Billie Burke, and the Lop-Eared Kid, also known as Charley Wilson. All burglars and cracksmen; and Rube Burrows, Colonel Carl Hobbgood and Captain Eugene Bunch, train robber who operated mostly in Louisiana, Mississippi and Alabama. Bunch was also a firearms expert and when in New Orleans usually passed as a Texas sheriff, spending most of his time in gun stores. Of all these criminals, only the Artful Dodger and Jack Cannon's luck ran out in New Orleans. The Dodger was sentenced to five years in 1896, and Cannon got two years in 1886, for robbery of the Royal and Gregg Hotels where he stole $8,000 in diamonds from a woman in May Banker's house on Union Street. Burrows was killed at Linden, Alabama in 1890 by Detective John McDuffie of Southeastern Express Company. Hobbgood and Bunch were cornered near Franlinton, Louisiana on August 22, 1892. Bunch was killed and Hobbgood surrendered. Bunch's most notable exploit was the single-handed robbery of a train on the Queen and Crescent Railway, near Derby, Mississippi on November 3, 1881 when he took $28,000 from the express car.

There were numerous local gangs of thieves headed by Yellow Henry Stewart, Irish Hoolihan, Monk O'Brien, Willie Walla, and Phil Oster. The worst of the lot was Yellow Henry's mob. A smaller gang known as the Spiders was just as dangerous. They had a house (hangout) on Franklin Street near Poydras which they called the Web. They specialized in robbing the Negro gambling houses, many of which paid them a weekly sum for protection. In the 1884 city elections the Spiders were used by the Guillotte Machine as bullies, but two years later, having outlived their usefulness to the politician, the Web was raided and hounded out of business. For several months the hangout was occupied by Margaret Murphy, who had been a pickpocket for more than sixty years mostly operating at funerals. When she was finally captured in 1887 at the age of seventy-seven, she boasted that during the two years prior to her arrest she had picked more than a hundred pockets. Phil Oster was an expert counterfeiter. He began making money at age twenty-five and continued for almost fifty years. Oster was last heard of in New Orleans in November 1917. He was seventy-one years old when secret service men found counterfeiting apparatus in his room on Bourbon Street. Oster had this to say to the States reporter:

"I've been in the penitentiary five times. I've been pardoned as many times, and I am proud of my record. I started making counterfeit money forty-five years ago. It took them fifteen years before they got me, and after I had made and spent enough money - if I had it now, well, there would be few, if any, men in New Orleans more wealthy".

Yellow Henry's gang membership included some of the most desperate and dangerous criminals that the New Orleans Underworld has yet produced. Any one of these characters could hold their own and feel perfectly at home in the Swamp or the infamous Gallatin Street when those districts were at their toughest. Among them were Crooked Neck Delany, Joe John, George Sylvester, Garibaldi Balden; Joe Martin, an expert garroter; Prussian Charley Mader, who always wore a mask and a false beard when working; George Lehde, Pat Keeley, Jim Maroney; Tom McDonald, better known as Tom the Dog; the Haley Brother, Red and Blue; and the notorious Frank Lyons, who is said to have been the son of Jack Lyons of Gallatin Street fame. Yellow Henry became leader of the gang in 1877 when the former leader Turpo went to prison for ten years. In 1884 Yellow Henry, Lyons, Sylvester and Balden went to prison for the robbery of a Julia St. Sailmaker. Sylvester died in the Parish prison, but the others were sent to the State Penitentiary, where Yellow Henry died in July 1886, of malaria. Lyons escaped in 1888, but was soon returned to prison and remained there until he was pardoned by Governor Nicholls in 1890. He then reorganized the Yellow Henry gang. In 1892 he killed Patrolman John Hurley for trying to stop a fight at Gallatin and Hospital Streets. A few months later he was sentenced to prison for life.

Joseph Shakespeare became Mayor in the spring of 1888 (he had previously filled that office from 1880 to 1882) on a somewhat reform ticket. Shakespeare appointed David Hennessy Chief of Police. Hennessy was marked for death by the Stoppagherra, a branch of the Mafia, the notorious Sicilian murder society.

These Sicilian criminals appeared in New Orleans after the beginning of the wave of immigration from Southern Europe before the Civil War and within a few years were operating in well organized bands in parts of the City. In June of 1861 the True Delta announced that "recent developments have satisfied the police of the City that an organized gang of Spanish and Sicilian thieves and burglars have long made their headquarters in the Second and Third Districts". Two months later the same newspaper reported the arrest of a band of Sicilian counterfeiters. In March of 1869 the Times said that the Second District was infested by "well-known and notorious Sicilian murderers, counterfeiters and burglars, who, in the last month, have formed a sort of general co-partnership or stock company for the plunder and disturbance of the City". This "partnership" was the Stoppagherra Society, organized as a branch of the Mafia by four men who, driven from Palermo by the Sicilian authorities, arrived in New Orleans early in 1869. The assassins of the Stoppagherra quickly disposed of a gang of Messina men who attempted to set up a rival band in the Autumn of 1869, and thereafter the Mafia was the dominating element in Italian crime, not only in New Orleans but elsewhere in the United States.

With New Orleans as headquarters, branches were soon established in New York, San Francisco, Chicago and other large cities. With the help of politicians who found the Mafia a great help at election time, a stream of criminals from Sicily found their way to the United States. In New Orleans alone during the late 1880's, according to the Italian Consul, Pasquale Conte,[1] there were a hundred escaped Italian criminals - not one of whom had entered the United States of America legally. Many had become naturalized citizens, those dangerous men and other members of the Mafia kept the Italian Colony of New Orleans in a state of terror for more than twenty years, and became rich and powerful plying their trades of robbery, extortion, and assassinations. Many of their victims were their own countrymen. About seventy killings were committed with knives, during the twenty years but most of them were done with a weapon known as the "Mafia gun" - a sawed off shot gun specially designed to be carried under the coat. While the Mafia was gaining a foothold in New Orleans, the head of the society in Sicily was a man named Leoni and his chief lieutenant was Guiseppi Esposito, who was notorious for his cruelty. In 1880 Leoni and his band, operating near Palermo, captured an English Clergy, the Reverend Mr. Rose and when no ransom came they cut off his ears and sent them to his family. The British government made such a demand upon Italy that troops were dispatched. Leoni was killed and many of his men captured, but Esposita and six others escaped and were smuggled aboard a ship bound for the United States. In March 1881, Esposito came to New Orleans where he rented a house on Chartres Street, assumed the name of Radzo and bought a small boat which he used in the oyster trade between New Orleans and the Southern Gulf Coast. He named the boat Leoni.

When Esposito arrived in New Orleans, the head of the local Mafia, according to the best information from police files, was Tony Labruzzo. He was immediately deposed by Esposito, who extorted money from wealthy Italians and began a Sicilian-style organization, with a fleet of boats and a hide-away in the swamps where he could hold his victims for ransoms. His plan never matured. Labruzzo, bitter because of his loss of power, informed the Italian Consul that the escaped bandit was in New Orleans. The Consul notified the Chief of Police. Through the

---

[1]   In an interview with the New York Tribune, quoted in the American Law Review, May-June 1891.

combined efforts of the local authorities and Consul, Esposito was captured on July 5,1881 in Jackson Square. The next morning he was put aboard a ship for New York. From New York Esposito was sent to Italy where he was imprisoned in irons for the remainder of his life. Ten years after Esposito's arrest Labruzzo was shot dead in Bienville Street by a Mafioso named Guitano Ardatta. Both Mike and David Hennessy (police officials) were warned by the Society to prepare for death. Mike was killed in Houston five years later. It was ten years before the Society carried out its threats of vengeance against David.

Soon after the capture of Esposito and the assassination of Labruzzo, the Mafia in New Orleans came under the leadership of Charles Matranga and his brother Tony. While the actual strength and inner workings of the Organization were never known, the police believed that by 1885 the Mafia were at least three hundred in number and Tony Matranga was president and that it was governed by a supreme council of twenty which prepared the extortion letters, planned the murders and assigned the assassins.

Around the beginning of the twentieth century, the Mafia was showing signs of loosing its grip (so to speak) on New Orleans. Its presence was still of paramount concern by both city officials and residents.

To adequately and completely describe the devastating impact that criminals had on the City of New Orleans would simply bankrupt the English language.

Epilogue

On December 14, 1997, a national television network, CBS, broadcast an investigative report, hosted by Ed Bradley, live entitled, "New Orleans Cops". The report was a segment of the program called <u>60 Minutes</u> and was hosted by Ed Bradley.

It revealed law enforcement officers heavily engaged in criminal activities including murder. A new Chief of Police, with outside specialists from New York City, is reported to be currently making discernable progress in eradicating the corruption.

Stay Tuned

About the Author

Fred deClouet came to Denver in 1964 as an employee in the education department of the U.S Justice Department Bureau of Prison's. He retired as a Media Production offer/Educator in 1984

His professional background encompasses various responsible capacities e.g Small Business Administration (SBA) counseling, research and writing, consulting and corporate management.

As an author Fred has produced works on Adult Basic Education, Occupational Educational Curricula, Personal Recruitment, Equal Opportunities and Instructional television and Educational Media. Fred designed, built and implemented a closed circuit television system to support the Justice Department's overall education treatment program. He also taught a television production course of study.

His Authorship includes the following:
1. An auditing guide fort he U.S Justice Department.
2. Co-authored with Lantry & Switzer, (Colorado State University) <u>Selection</u> of <u>Production Technique</u> for <u>Instruction Television</u>. His general background includes Regional (5state) Director of the International Industrial Television Association and Vice President of Group Fifty (50) Corporation. A prepaid legal services company with offices in several states.

Author of system and curriculum studies (University of Hawaii) supported by federal grants. Fred also authored articles published in professional journals, e.g <u>Business Law Forum</u> and Personal Journal.

Fred, a World War II retired U.S Marine, is the author of <u>First Black Marines, and account</u> of <u>Blacks in the Marine Corps, Winston Derex Publisher, 1995.</u>

The following are excerpts from reviewers of thebook.

1. "Fred deClouet has turned out a real gem, It's a fine addition to my library "C.F Mundy, Commandant of the U.S Marine Corps.

2. It's his focus on historical information that highlights deClouet's writing Dr. Z. Bolden, New Orleans Tribune.

3. "deClouet documents the contributions and sacrifice of Black Marines in the WWII effort. "Well researched." Greater Park Hill News - Denver.

4. "The Author takes you through the war zone of emotions and resulting back lash in the Military's effort to integrate itself." Ed Curlie. The Urban Spectrum Newspaper.